Table of Cont

The Heart Of A Dog

Mikhail Bulgakov

Introduction

The Heart Of A Dog is a Russian Frankenstein tale with a gentle twist and a happy end. A kindly professor performs a daring experiment to turn a dog into a human being by transplanting human organs into it; the result is hilarious social satire and a condemnation of revolution and the new communist state.

Mikhail Bulgakov (1891–1940) suffered at the hands of the Soviet system. His family, educated and religious, managed to emigrate to France. As a doctor in the First World War and later during the Civil War, he could not. His life's vicissitudes made it difficult for him to survive as a writer: after performing a tracheotomy on a child in 1917 he contracted diphtheria, which he treated with morphine and soon found himself addicted. He went through three marriages and battled constantly with Soviet censorship. Partly because of the latter, his masterpiece *The Master and Margarita* was not published until 1966, and the manuscript of *The Heart Of A Dog* was confiscated in 1926, shortly after it was written, and not published until forty years later by a Russian-language press in Germany.

He had some successes, most notably the play *Days of the Turbins* (1926), based on his novel *The White Guard* (1924), about the family of an officer who fought against the Red Army in the civil war that tore Russia apart for years after the Bolshevik Revolution of 1917. The play was produced by Konstantin Stanislavsky at the famed Moscow Art Theatre only with the permission of Stalin, who loved it and attended almost every performance. Yet Stalin would neither allow Bulgakov to produce his play *Batum* about the dictator's youth, nor to publish any of his prose. Nor would Stalin permit Bulgakov to join his family abroad. Despair and stress exacerbated his kidney disease and the writer died in 1940.

Bulgakov's early prose included some science fiction and fantasy. The genre is an excellent medium for social satire. Often, censors do not recognize the hidden references or, perhaps, pretend not to see. Two short stories, 'Diaboliad' and 'The Fatal Eggs', were published, and Bulgakov intended the next novella to be in the same genre. Prior to submitting *The Heart Of A Dog* for publication, Bulgakov read the new work aloud to a small group in March 1925. Naturally, there were quite perceptive police spies in the audience. One reported that the work mocked the proletariat, rejected terror as a means of changing people and denied all the achievements of the Soviet system. It was also, he wrote, luridly pornographic, under the guise of being scientific. He concluded: "I believe that the censors will not permit its publication. But this book has been read to an audience of forty-eight people, ninety per cent of whom are themselves writers. Thus its role, its main work, has been accomplished: it has infected the writers' minds and will sharpen their quills." The novella was banned.

Professor Preobrazhensky, a "high priest of science", is a godlike character who works on the rejuvenation of the ageing rich in order to discover the secrets of life. His disdain for the Soviet regime and *Homo socialisticus* is expressed strongly and frankly, creating problems with the new Bolsheviks running his apartment building, a quartet of fervent revolutionaries blinded by ideology and stupidity.

The narrative of *The Heart Of A Dog* combines several points of view, often shifting at unexpected moments: it begins with the stray dog's story of misery, licking its wounds in an alley during a blizzard, watching a young woman fight her way through the storm—for a brief moment we "tune in" on her thoughts and fears. Then the dog is picked up and led away by a well-dressed bourgeois gentleman, Professor Preobrazhensky—the dog can tell proletarians from the bourgeoisie easily. The descriptions of the luxurious apartment-cum-office, the faithful assistant, Dr Bormental, the maid and the cook are all filtered through the limited understanding of the canine mind. The narrative is continued by Dr Bormental, who keeps the case notes of the historic and God-challenging operation and recovery. Then we see things from the perspective of the new man, Sharikov, as he becomes more and more Bolshevik and anti-bourgeois, more and more radical and stupid.

These intentional shifts in angle are disorienting, as are the changes in register and vocabulary. Often it is not clear at first who is speaking or what about. But a few lines later, we see what Bulgakov wants us to see.

Preobrazhensky is now a classic character, frequently quoted by Russians. Witty, acerbic, cultured and scholarly, he is full of theories about enjoying life. He delivers a wonderful lecture on how to eat and drink properly, the main rule being: do not read Soviet newspapers before meals. He represents everything the revolutionary regime wants to eradicate, just as Sharikov is the embodiment of everything that is ruining Russia in the professor's view. To him, the Soviet culture is dumbing down the country, filling people's heads with talk of equality and rebellion instead of instilling the virtues of hard work and education.

The professor has no patience with committees and regulations, and resents the attempts to turn his commodious apartment into a communal flat.
Bulgakov's tale is imbued with religious and musical symbolism and allusions. This story of the birth of a new man takes place between late December 1924 and early January 1925; that is, between Christmas Eve on the Western calendar and Christmas Eve on the Russian Orthodox calendar. The religious underpinnings appear in the proper names: "Preobrazhensky" comes from the Russian "*Preobrazheniye*" ("Transfiguration") and is a common surname among the clergy. The Arbat area where the action takes place has lanes with names like Myortvy ("Dead") and Prechistenka ("Holy"). The professor is an opera-lover, and he sings the chorus "To the Sacred Banks of the Nile" from *Aida* when he is under stress. A new production of *Aida* entered the repertory of the Bolshoi Opera Theatre in 1922. The chorus is sung to strengthen the resolve of the Egyptian army and to aid the warrior Radames in his quest to transform the simple slave girl Aida into his legitimate wife when he becomes a commander. The first encounter with the opera is in the story's opening pages, when the stray dog grumbles about "the old biddy who sings in the moonlight—'Celeste Aida'" (that is, "Heavenly Aida", which is Radames's love aria). When the professor is in a more cheerful mood, he likes to sing *Don Juan's Serenade*, a romance composed by Tchaikovsky to a poem by Alexei Tolstoy. In it, Don Juan entreats the lovely Nisetta to come out on her balcony so that he can play his guitar for her.
The Heart Of A Dog is incredibly accurate about Moscow in those two weeks: the references to the playbills, the circus acts listed in the newspaper, the performance of the opera and the weather are exactly right, almost as in a diary.
Many of the characters are recognizable as well. The prototype for the professor is Bulgakov's uncle, a professor of medicine and a gynaecologist. Some of Preobrazhensky's patients were well-known to readers at the time: Moritz (the young lover of a woman seeking rejuvenation) was a man-about-town whose many affairs were grist for the gossip mill; the political official with a predilection for young women was recognizable and the censors first deleted all reference to him before banning the work completely.
The "new man" created by the professor is a parody of the "new man" meant to evolve under the Soviet system. Sharikov becomes a monster who turns on his creator under the influence of socialist propaganda;

frighteningly, it becomes clear that Sharikov is bound to turn on his revolutionary teachers as well. A terrible force is unleashed.

Thus, *The Heart Of A Dog* deftly combines reality and fact with fiction and fantasy. The main hero, the mutt Sharik, becomes the main villain, the upstart Sharikov. Full of remorse, Professor Preobrazhensky takes it upon himself to play God once again and reverses the operation. Peace is restored to the apartment, but the social experiment outside his windows continued until the end of the twentieth century.

The Heart Of A Dog
A Monstrous Story

Chapter 1

Aooooo-ooow-ooow! O, look at me, I'm dying! The blizzard in the alley is roaring a dirge for me, and I'm howling with it. I'm done for, gone! The bastard in the filthy cap—the cook in the normalized nutrition canteen serving the Central Economic Council—sloshed boiling water at me and burned my left side. What a creep, and a proletarian to boot! Lord, God almighty, it hurts! The boiling water ate through to the bone. So I howl and howl and howl, but how can howling help?

What did I ever do to him? What? Did he think I'd eat the Economic Council out of its stores if I rummaged in the rubbish? Greedy creature. Take a look at his mug some time: fat, broad cheeks. He's a brass faced thief. People, help! The white-hat gave me a taste of boiling water at noon; now it's dark, around four in the afternoon, going by the onion smell from the Prechistenka fire station. The firemen get buckwheat groats for dinner, as you well know. But that's way down on my list, like mushrooms. Dogs I know from Prechistenka told me, however, that there's a place called The Bar on Neglinny Street, where people gobble up the special of the day, mushrooms *en sauce piquante*, at three roubles seventy-five a portion. To each his own—for me it's like licking galoshes... Oooow... My side is killing me, and I can see my future career absolutely clearly: tomorrow there will be sores and I'd like to know how I'm supposed to treat them. In the summer you can go down to Sokolniki Park, there's a particularly good grass there, and besides which, you can stuff yourself with sausage ends and the citizenry litter the place with greasy wrapping paper that's good to lick. And if not for some old biddy who sings in the moonlight—'Celeste Aida'*—in a way that turns your stomach, all would be fine. But now where am I supposed to go? Have you been kicked by boots? Yes. Have you ever got a brick in the ribs? Plenty of times. I've suffered it all, I've accepted my fate, and if I'm crying now it's only from the physical pain and the hunger, because my spirit hasn't dimmed yet... The canine spirit is very tenacious. But my body is broken, battered, people have had their fun with it. The worst part is this: once he'd poured the boiling water on me, it ate through the fur, and now there's no protection for my left side. I could easily get pneumonia, and if I do, citizens, I will starve to death. When you have pneumonia, you're supposed to lie under the main stairs inside, and who's going to run around the bins in search of food except me, a bedridden bachelor dog? If my lung is affected, I'll be crawling on my belly, weakened, and any guy with a stick can finish me off. And then the street-cleaners with their badges will grab me by my legs and toss me into their cart...

Of all the proletarians, street-cleaners are the vilest scum. Human dregs, the lowest category. You get different kinds of cooks. Take the late Vlas from Prechistenka. How many lives he saved! The most important thing when you're sick is to get a bite. And there were times, the old hounds say, when Vlas would toss a bone and it would have an ounce of meat on it. May he rest in peace for being a real human being, the personal chef to the Count Tolstoys, and not from the Council of Normalized Nutrition. What they do in the name of normalized nutrition is beyond a dog's mind to understand! Those bastards use rotten corned beef to make cabbage soup, and the poor customers know nothing about it. They come, eat, guzzle it down!

This little typist of the ninth rank earns forty-five roubles but, of course, her lover gives her fine cotton stockings. And how much she has to put up with for those *fil de Perse* stockings! He doesn't just take her the usual way, he makes her do it French style. Real bastards, those French, just between you and me. Though they eat well, all washed down with red wine. Yes... So the little typist will come to eat there, she can't afford to go to The Bar on forty-five roubles! She doesn't have enough for the movies, and movies are the sole consolation for women. She shudders and winces but eats it. Just think, forty copecks for two courses, while both those courses don't even cost fifteen, because the manager steals the remaining twenty-five copecks. And is this the kind of food she should be eating? The tip of her right lung has a spot, and she has women's troubles thanks to that French stuff, they docked her wages at work and fed her putrid meat at the canteen, there she is, there she is! Running into the alley in her lover's stockings. Her feet are cold, the wind is blowing on her belly because her fur's like mine, and she wears cold undies, just a lacy appearance of underwear. Tatters for her lover. Let her try putting on flannel pants. He'll shout: "Why can't you be sexy? I'm sick and tired of my Matryona, sick of her flannel underpants, my time has come. I'm a chairman now, and everything I embezzle goes to female flesh, chocolates and bottles of Abrau-Durso!* I spent my entire youth hungry, I'm done with that, and there is no afterlife."

I pity her, I do. But I pity myself even more. That's not my egoism talking, oh no, but it's because we truly are in unequal conditions. At least she's warm at home, but what about me? Where can I go? Beaten, scalded, spat upon, where can I go? Ooooow-ooow!

"Here, boy. Sharik, come on, Sharik! Why are you whining, poor thing? Eh? Did someone hurt you?... Ooof!"
The blizzard wind, that witch, rattled the gates and smacked the young lady on the ear with its broom. It lifted her skirt to her knees, revealing creamy stockings and a narrow strip of poorly laundered lace underwear, stifling her words and sweeping away the dog.
My God, what terrible weather... Ooof... And my stomach aches. That salted meat! When will it all end?
Lowering her head, the young woman launched herself into the attack, breaking through the gates, and she was spun round and round, tossed and then twisted into a snowy funnel, before she vanished.
The dog remained near the alley, suffering the pain of his mutilated side, pressed himself against the cold wall, held his breath and decided that he would never leave this spot again, that he would die right there. Despair overwhelmed him. He felt such bitterness and pain, such loneliness and fear, that tiny canine tears bubbled from his eyes and dried on the spot. His fur on the wounded side was all in shredded, frozen clumps, revealing vicious red burns. How stupid, nasty and cruel were cooks. She called him "Sharik"...* What the hell kind of "Sharik" was he! Sharik was a fluffball, a round, well-fed, dumb, oatmeal-eating son of pedigree parents, and he was a shaggy, bony and scruffy stray, a homeless dog. But thanks for the kind thought.
The door of the brightly lit shop across the road slammed, and a citizen appeared. A citizen, not a comrade, and probably a gentleman. As he came closer, it was clear he was a gentleman. Don't you think I judge by the overcoat. Nonsense. Lots of proles wear overcoats now too. Of course, not with collars like that, no way, but still you could get confused from a distance. But I judge by the eyes—you can't mistake them either near or far! Oh, eyes are a significant thing! Like a barometer. You can see everything—who has a vast desert in his heart, who can jab you in the ribs with the toe of his boot for no reason at all, and who is afraid of everything. There's such pleasure in nipping the last type in the calf. Afraid? So there. If you're afraid, you deserve it. Grrrrr... arf!
The gentleman crossed the street confidently in the column of blowing snow and moved towards the gate. Yes, yes, I could see everything about him. He wouldn't put away that putrid corned beef, and if anyone dared serve him some he would raise such a fuss and write to the papers saying: "They gave me, Filipp Filippovich, rotten meat!"
Here he comes, closer and closer. This one eats well and doesn't steal. He won't kick you, but he's not afraid of anyone, and that's because

he's never hungry. He is a gentleman who does intellectual labour, with a French pointy beard and a grey moustache, fluffy and dashing, like French knights had, but the blizzard carries his smell and it's a bad one—hospital and cigar.

What the hell brings him to the Central Economy Co-op? Now he's right there... What's he looking for? Oh-oh... What could he want to buy in that crummy little store, aren't the fancy stores on Okhotny Ryad* enough? What is it?! Sausage. Mister, if you saw how they made that sausage you wouldn't go anywhere near the store. Give it to me!

The dog mustered what little strength it had and madly crawled out from beneath the gate onto the pavement. The blizzard thundered like a rifle shot above him, billowing the huge letters on a canvas poster: "IS REJUVENATION POSSIBLE?"

Of course it is. The smell rejuvenated me, got me up off my belly, raising fiery waves in my stomach that had been empty for two days, the smell vanquished the hospital, the heavenly fragrance of ground mare with garlic and pepper.

I can smell it, I know he's got sausage in his right pocket. He's standing above me. O, master! Look at me. I am dying. We've got slaves' hearts, a miserable fate!

The dog crawled like a snake on its belly, streaming tears. Note the cook's work. But you're not going to give me any. Oh, I know rich people very well! Yet, essentially, what do you want it for? What do you want with rotten horsemeat? You won't get poison like this anywhere except at the Moscow Agricultural Processing Trust, that's for sure. You had breakfast today, you world luminary, thanks to male sex glands. Oooo-oooh... What is going on in this fair world? I guess it's too early to die, and despair is a sin. I have to lick his hands, there's nothing else left to do.

The mysterious gentleman bent over the dog, the gold frames around his eyes glinting, and took a long white package out of his right pocket. Without taking off his brown gloves, he unwrapped the paper, which the storm immediately took away, and broke off a piece of sausage, which was called Cracow Special. And gave the piece to the dog. Oh, what a selfless individual! Oooh—ooh!

"*Phweet*," the gentleman whistled and added in a stern voice, "Here! Sharik, Sharik!"

Sharik again. I've been baptized. Call me whatever you want. In return for your exceptional act...

The dog instantly pulled off the casing, clamped onto the Cracow sausage with a slurp and gulped it down in a trice. And choked on the

sausage and snow to the point of tears, because he had almost swallowed the string in his greed. More, I lick your hand more. I kiss your trousers, my benefactor!
"Enough for now..." The gentleman spoke in short bursts, as if giving orders. He leant over Sharik, looked interrogatively into his eyes and unexpectedly ran his gloved hand intimately and gently over Sharik's belly.
"Ah-ha," he said portentously, "no collar, that's lovely, you're just the one I want. Follow me." He clicked his fingers.
"Phweet!"
Follow you? To the ends of the earth. You can kick me with your suede shoes and I won't say a word.
Street lamps glowed all over Prechistenka. His side ached terribly, but Sharik sometimes forgot about it, lost in one thought only—how not to lose in the crowd the miraculous vision in a fur coat, and how to express his love and loyalty. And he expressed it some seven times down the length of Prechistenka to Obukhov Lane. He kissed his shoe; near Myortvy Lane, trying to clear the path, he scared some lady with his wild bark so much that she sank down on an advertising pillar; and once or twice he whined to maintain the man's pity.
Some bitch of a stray cat, looking like a Siberian, slipped out of a drain pipe, having caught the scent of the sausage despite the blizzard. Sharik almost lost his mind at the prospect that this rich weirdo who picked up wounded dogs in doorways would pick up this thief too, and he would have to share the processed meat. He snarled and bared his teeth at the cat, and the feline hissed like a hole-riddled water hose, and climbed up the pipe to the second floor. Grrrrrrr... arf! Scat! You can't stock up enough from the processing centre for all the freeloaders hanging around on Prechistenka.
The gentleman appreciated the loyalty and right at the fire station, by the window that emitted the pleasant grumble of a French horn, rewarded the dog with a second piece about an ounce smaller.
Silly man. Luring me. Don't worry! I'm not going off on my own. I'll follow you wherever you go.
"*Phweet!* This way!"
Onto Obukhov? By all means. We know this lane very well.
Phweet!
This way? With pleas—oh, no, sorry. There's a doorman. There's nothing worse than a doorman. Much more dangerous than a street-cleaner. An absolutely hateful breed. More disgusting than cats. A flayer in gold braid.

"Don't be afraid. Go."
"Good evening, Filipp Filippovich."
"Hello, Fyodor."
Now there's a personality for you. My God, what have you found for me, my dog's destiny! What kind of man is this who can bring dogs off the street past doormen into an apartment building run by a council of comrades? Look at that scoundrel—not a word, not a movement! His eyes look disturbed, but in general he is indifferent under his gold-braided cap. As if this is how things should be. That's respect, gentlemen, real respect. Well, and I'm with him and behind him. What, touch me? Here's a bite. I'd love to sink my teeth into your calloused proletarian foot. For all the torment from your brethren. How many times did you poke my face with a broom, eh?
"Come on, come on."
I got it, don't worry. Wherever you go, so do I. You just show me the way, and I'll keep up, despite my miserable side.
Calling down from the stairs: "Were there any letters for me, Fyodor?"
From below, respectfully: "No sir, Filipp Filippovich, there weren't"—then, in an intimate, low tone, adding—"they've moved new tenants into apartment three."
The important canine benefactor turned abruptly on the step, leant over the banister, and asked in horror, "Really?"
His eyes opened wide and his moustache bristled.
The doorman tilted his head, brought his hand to his mouth and confirmed it. "Yes sir, a total of four of them."
"My God! I can just imagine the state of the apartment now. And what did they say?"
"Nothing."
"And Fyodor Pavlovich?"
"He went out for screens and bricks. To make partitions."
"I'll be damned!"
"They'll be moving people into all the apartments, Filipp Filippovich, except yours. There was a meeting; they elected a new council of comrades and sent the old one packing."
"The goings-on. Ai-ai-ai... *Phweet.*"
I'm on my way, hurrying. My side is making itself felt, you see. Allow me to lick your boot.
The doorman's gold braid vanished below. The marble landing was warm from the pipes, we turned one more time and reached the first floor.

Chapter 2

There's absolutely no reason to learn how to read when you can smell meat a mile away. Nevertheless, if you live in Moscow and you have a modicum of sense in your head, you learn some reading willy-nilly, and without taking any courses. Of the forty thousand Moscow dogs there must only be one total idiot who can't make out the word "sausage" syllable by syllable. Sharik started learning by colour. He had just turned four months when they hung greenish blue signs all over Moscow with the words "MSPO Meat Trade". We repeat, none of that is needed because you can smell meat anyway. And there was some confusion once: going by the toxic blue colour, Sharik, whose nose was masked by the petrol fumes of cars, ran into the Golubizner Brothers' electrical-goods shop on Myasnitskaya Street instead of a butcher shop. There, at the brothers' shop, the dog felt the sting of insulated wire, which is a lot tougher than a coachman's whip. That famous moment should be considered the start of Sharik's education. Back on the pavement, Sharik immediately understood that "blue" doesn't always mean "meat" and, tucking his tail between his hind legs and howling with pain, he recalled that all the butchers' signs started on the left with a gold or reddish squat squiggle that looks like a sled: "M".

Things went more successfully after that. He learnt "A" from "Glavryba", the fish store on the corner of Mokhovaya, and then the "B" (because it was easier to run over from the tail end of the word for fish, "*ryba*", since there always was a policeman standing at the beginning of the word).

Tile squares on the façades of corners in Moscow always and inevitably meant "Cheese". The black tap of a samovar (the letter "Ch") that started the word stood for the former owner Chichkin, mountains of Dutch red cheese, vicious salesmen who hated dogs, sawdust on the floor and the most vile, stinky Backstein cheese.

If someone was playing a concertina—which wasn't much better than 'Celeste Aida'—and it smelt of hotdogs, the first letters on the white signs quite conveniently formed the word "Foul..." which meant: "Foul language not permitted and no tipping." Here brawls cycloned sporadically, people were punched in the face—albeit rarely—while dogs were beaten continually with napkins or boots.

If the windows displayed leathery hanging hams and piles of mandarin oranges, it was a delicatessen. If there were dark bottles with a bad liquid, it was a woof, wow... w...ine store. The former Yeliseyev Brothers' store.

The unknown gentleman, who had lured the dog to the door of his luxurious apartment on the second floor, rang and the dog looked up at the big card, black with gold letters, hanging to the side of the wide door with panes of wavy, rosy glass. He combined the first three letters right away: puh-ar-o—"Pro". But then came a tubby, double-sided bitch of a letter that didn't stand for anything he knew.*

"Could it be proletariat?" wondered Sharik doubtfully. "That can't be." He raised his nose and sniffed the fur coat once again, and thought confidently: "No, there's no smell of the proletariat here. It's a scholarly word, and God only knows what it means."

Behind the rosy glass an unexpected and joyful light came on, casting the black card deeper into shadow. The door opened without a sound and a pretty young woman in a white apron and lace cap appeared before dog and man. The former was enveloped in divine warmth, and the woman's skirt gave off the scent of lily of the valley.

"Now you're talking, this is it," thought the dog.

"Please enter, Mr Sharik," the man invited sarcastically, and Sharik entered reverently, tail wagging.

A great number of objects cluttered the rich entrance. The floor-length mirror that instantly reflected the second bedraggled and scruffy Sharik, the scary antlers up high, the endless fur coats and rubber boots and the opal tulip with electricity on the ceiling—all stuck in his head immediately.

"Where did you pick up this one, Filipp Filippovich?" asked the woman with a smile and helped him remove his heavy coat, lined with dark-brown fox with a bluish tinge. "Lord! What a mangy thing!"

"Nonsense. Where is he mangy?" the gentleman asked severely and gruffly.

Upon removing his fur coat, he appeared in a black suit of English cloth, and a gold chain twinkled happily and subtly across his belly.

"Just wait, stop wriggling, *phweet*... stop twisting, silly. Hmmm... That's not mange... will you stand still, damn you!... Hmmm... Ah! It's a burn. What bastard scalded you? Eh? Stand still, will you!"

"The cook, the criminal. The cook!" The dog spoke with his piteous eyes and whined a bit.

"Zina," ordered the man, "bring him to the examining room and me my coat!"

The woman whistled and clicked her fingers and the dog, after a brief hesitation, followed her. Together, they entered a narrow, dimly lit

corridor, passed a lacquered door and came to the end, and then went left and ended up in a dark cubbyhole, which instantly displeased the dog by its evil smell. The darkness clicked and turned into blinding daylight, and it sparkled, lit up, and turned white from all sides.
"Oh, no," the dog howled mentally, "sorry, not for me! I get it! Damn them and their sausage! They've lured me into a dog hospital. They'll force me to eat castor oil and they'll cut up my side with knives, and it hurts too much to touch as it is!"
"Hey, no! Where do you think you're going!" shouted the one called Zina.
The dog twisted away, coiled up, and then hit the door with its healthy side so hard that the whole apartment shuddered. Then he flew back, spun around in place like a top, and knocked over a white bucket that scattered clumps of cotton wool. As he spun, walls flew by, fitted with cupboards of gleaming instruments, and the white apron and distorted female face jumped up.
"Where are you going, you shaggy devil!" Zina shouted desperately. "Damn you!"
"Where's the back stairs?" thought the dog. He reversed and smashed himself against the glass, hoping that it was a second door. A cloud of glass shards flew out with thunder and ringing, a tubby jar with reddish crap jumped out, spilling all over the floor and stinking up the room. The real door swung open.
"Stop! B-bastard!" The man shouted, jumping around in his white coat with only one sleeve on, and grabbed the dog by its legs. "Zina, hold him by the scruff of his neck, the scoundrel!"
"Wow! What a dog!"
The door opened even wider and another person of the male gender in a white coat burst in. Crushing broken glass, he rushed not towards the dog but the cupboard, opened it, and the whole room was filled with a sweet and nauseating odour. Then the person fell onto the dog with his belly, and the dog took pleasure in nipping him above the shoelaces. The person gasped but held on. The nauseating liquid filled the dog's breathing and everything in his head spun, then he couldn't feel his legs and he slid off somewhere sideways, crookedly.
"Thanks, it's over," he thought dreamily, falling right on the sharp pieces of glass, "farewell, Moscow! I'll never see Chichkin and proletarians and Cracow sausages again! I'm going to Heaven for my canine suffering. Fellows, knackers, why did you do me in?"
And then he fell over on his side completely and croaked.

When he was resurrected, his head spun lightly and he had a bit of nausea in his belly, but it was if he had no side; his side was deliciously silent. The dog half-opened his right eye and out of the corner saw that he was tightly bandaged across his sides and belly. "They had their way after all, the sons-of-bitches," he thought woozily, "but cleverly, you have to give them that."

"From Seville to Granada... in the quiet twilight of the nights,"* a distracted falsetto voice sang above him.

The dog was surprised; he opened both eyes fully and saw two steps away from him a man's foot on a white stool. The trouser leg and long underpants were hiked up and the bare yellow shin was smeared with dried blood and iodine.

"Saints alive!" thought the dog. "That must be where I bit him. My work. They'll whip me now!"

"'Serenades abound, swords clash all around!' Why did you bite a doctor, you mutt? Eh? Why did you break the glass? Eh?"

"Ooo-ooo-ooo," the dog whimpered piteously.

"Well, all right, you're conscious, so just lie there, you dummy."

"How did you manage to lure such a nervous dog, Filipp Filippovich?" asked a pleasant male voice, and the knit underpants slid down. Tobacco smoke filled the air, and glass bottles rattled in the cupboard.

"With kindness. It's the only way possible in dealing with a living creature. Terror won't work at all with an animal, at whatever level of development it may be. I've said it before and I say it again and will continue saying it. They're wrong to think that terror will help them. No, no, it won't, whatever its colour: white, red or even brown! Terror paralyses the nervous system completely. Zina! I bought this wastrel a rouble and forty copecks' worth of Cracow sausage. Be so kind as to feed him when he's no longer nauseated."

Broken glass tinkled as it was swept up, and a woman's voice noted flirtatiously: "Cracow sausage! God, you should have gotten him two copecks' worth of scraps at the butcher! I'll eat the Cracow sausage myself."

"Just try! I'll eat you! It's poison for the human stomach. A grown young woman and you're like a baby sticking all kinds of nasty things in your mouth. Don't you dare! I'm warning you, neither Doctor Bormental nor I will bother with you when you get the runs. 'Everyone who says that another is your match...'"

Soft staccato bells jingled throughout the apartment, and in the distance voices sounded frequently in the entrance. The telephone rang. Zina vanished.

Filipp Filippovich tossed his cigarette butt in the bucket, buttoned his coat, smoothed his luxurious moustache in the mirror on the wall and called the dog.

"*Phweet, phweet*... come on, come on, it's fine! Let's go receive."

The dog got up on unsteady legs, swayed and trembled, but quickly got his bearings and followed the fluttering coat-tails of Filipp Filippovich. Once again the dog crossed the narrow corridor, but now he saw that it was brightly lit from above. When the lacquered door opened, he followed Filipp Filippovich into the office, which blinded the dog with its interior. First of all, it was blazing with light: it burned on the plaster ornamented ceiling, it burned on the desk, it burned on the wall and in the cupboard glass. Light poured over a myriad of objects, of which the most amusing was an enormous owl, sitting on a branch on the wall.

"Stay," ordered Filipp Filippovich.

The carved door opposite opened and the bitten man came in, and now in the bright light revealed as a very handsome young fellow with a pointy beard, and handed over a piece of paper, muttering, "The previous..."

He vanished silently, while Filipp Filippovich smoothed the tails of his lab coat and sat behind the huge desk, thereby becoming incredibly important and imposing.

"No, this isn't a hospital, I've landed in some other place," the dog thought in confusion and flopped on the carpet by the heavy leather sofa, "and we'll figure out that owl too."

The door opened softly and someone came in, astonishing the dog enough to make him yap, but very diffidently.

"Quiet! Well, well, well! You're unrecognizable, dear fellow."

The newcomer bowed very respectfully and awkwardly to Filipp Filippovich.

"Hee-hee! You are a magician and sorcerer, professor," he muttered in embarrassment.

"Take off your pants, dear fellow," Filipp Filippovich commanded and stood up.

"Jesus!" thought the dog. "What a fruitcake!"

The fruitcake's head was covered with completely green hair, and at the back it had a rusty tobacco shimmer. Wrinkles spread out on the fruitcake's face, but his complexion was as pink as a baby's. His left leg couldn't bend and he had to drag it along the carpet, but the right one jerked like a toy nutcracker. On the lapel of his magnificent jacket, a precious stone protruded like an eye.

The dog was so interested that his nausea passed.
"Yip, yip," he barked softly.
"Quiet! How are you sleeping, dear fellow?"
"Hee-hee... Are we alone, professor? It's indescribable," the visitor said in embarrassment. "*Parole d'honneur*,* I've seen nothing like it for twenty-five years!" The subject touched the button of his trousers. "Can you believe it, Professor? Every night there are herds of naked girls... I am positively delighted. You are a sorcerer!"
"Hmmm," grunted Filipp Filippovich in concern, peering into his guest's pupils.
The latter had finally mastered the buttons and removed his striped trousers. Beneath them were unimaginable underpants. They were cream-coloured, with embroidered black silk cats, and they smelt of perfume. The dog couldn't resist the cats and barked, making the subject jump.
"Ai!"
"I'll whip you! Don't be afraid, he doesn't bite."
"I don't bite?" the dog was surprised.
A small envelope, with a picture of a beautiful girl with loosened tresses, fell out of the trousers pocket onto the floor. The subject jumped up, bent over, picked it up and blushed a deep red.
"You'd better watch it," Filipp Filippovich warned grimly, wagging his finger, "Do be careful not to abuse it!"
'I'm not abu..." the subject muttered in embarrassment, still undressing. "This was just an experiment, dear Professor."
"Well, and what were the results?" Filipp Filippovich asked sternly.
The subject waved his arm ecstatically.
"In twenty-five years, I swear to God, Professor, there was nothing like it! The last time was in 1899 in Paris on the Rue de la Paix."
"And why have you turned green?"
The visitor's face darkened.
"That damned Zhirkost!* You cannot imagine what those useless louts fobbed off on me instead of dye. Just look," he babbled, his eyes searching for a mirror. "It's terrible! They should be punched in the face," he added, growing angrier. "What I am supposed to do now, Professor?" he asked snivelling.
"Hm... Shave it all off."
"Professor!" the visitor exclaimed piteously, "It will grow back grey again! Besides which, I won't be able to show my face at work, I've been out three days now as it is. The car comes for me and I send it

away. Oh, Professor, if you could discover a way of rejuvenating hair as well!"
"Not right away, not right away, dear fellow," muttered Filipp Filippovich.
Bending over, he examined the patient's bare belly with glistening eyes. "Well, it's lovely, everything is perfectly fine... I didn't expect such a fine result, truth to tell... 'Lots of blood and lots of songs!'... Get dressed, dear fellow!"
"'And for the loveliest of all!...' the patient sang the next line in a voice as resonant as a frying pan and, glowing, started dressing. Having brought himself back to order, hopping and exuding perfume, he counted out a wad of white banknotes for Filipp Filippovich and tenderly pressed both of his hands.
"You need not return for two weeks," Filipp Filippovich said, "but I do ask that you be careful."
"Professor!" from beyond the door, in ecstasy, the guest exclaimed. "Do not worry in the least." He giggled sweetly and vanished.
The tinkling bell flew through the apartment, the lacquered door opened, the bitten one entered, handing Filipp Filippovich a piece of paper and announced: "The dates are incorrectly given. Probably 54–55. Heart tones low."
He vanished and was replaced by a rustling lady with a hat at a rakish angle and a sparkling necklace on her flabby and wrinkled neck. Terrible black bags sagged beneath her eyes, but her cheeks were a doll's rouge colour.
She was very agitated.
"Madam! How old are you?" Filipp Filippovich asked very severely.
The lady took flight and even paled beneath the crust of rouge.
"I, Professor... I swear, if you only knew, my drama..."
"How old, Madam?" Filipp Filippovich repeated even more severely.
"Honestly... well, forty-five—"
"Madam!" Filipp Filippovich cried out. "People are waiting! Don't hold me up, please, you are not the only one!"
The lady's bosom heaved mightily.
"I'll tell you alone, as a luminary of science, but I swear, it is so terrible—"
"How old are you?" Filipp Filippovich demanded angrily and squeakily, and his glasses flashed.
"Fifty-one," the lady replied, cowering in fear.
"Take off your pants, Madame," Filipp Filippovich said in relief and indicated a tall white scaffold in the corner.

"I swear, Professor," the lady muttered, undoing some snaps on her belt with trembling fingers, "That Moritz... I am confessing to you, hiding nothing..."
"'From Seville to Granada,'" Filipp Filippovich sang distractedly and stepped on the pedal under the marble sink. Water poured noisily.
"I swear to God!" the lady said, and live spots of colour broke through the artificial ones on her cheeks, "I know that this is my last passion... He's such a scoundrel! Oh, Professor! He's a card shark, all of Moscow knows it. He can't let a single lousy model get by. He's so devilishly young!" The lady mumbled and pulled out a crumpled lacy clump from beneath her rustling skirts.
The dog was completely confused and everything went belly up in his head.
"The hell with you," he thought dimly, resting his head on his paws and falling asleep from the shame, "I won't even try to understand what this is, since I won't get it anyway."
He was awaked by a ringing sound and saw that Filipp Filippovich had tossed some glowing tubes into a basin.
The spotted lady, pressing her hands to her breast, gazed hopefully at Filipp Filippovich. He frowned importantly and, sitting at his desk, made a notation.
"Madame, I will transplant ape ovaries in you," he announced and looked severe.
"Ah, Professor, must it be an ape?"
"Yes," Filipp Filippovich replied inexorably.
"When will the operation take place?" the lady asked in a weak voice, turning pale.
"'From Seville to Granada'... hm... Monday. You will check into the clinic in the morning and my assistant will prepare you."
"Ah, I don't want to be in the clinic. Can't you do it here, Professor?"
"You see, I do surgery here only in extreme situations. It will be very expensive, five thousand."
"I'm willing, Professor!"
The water thundered again, the feathered hat billowed, and then a head as bald as a plate appeared and embraced Filipp Filippovich. The dog dozed, the nausea had passed, and the dog enjoyed the calmed side and warmth, even snored a little and had time for a bit of a pleasant dream: he had torn a whole bunch of feathers from the owl's tail... Then an agitated voice bleated overhead:
"I am a well-known figure, Professor! What do I do now?"

"Gentlemen!" Filipp Filippovich shouted in outrage. "You can't behave this way! You have to control yourself! How old is she?"
"Fourteen, Professor... You realize that the publicity will destroy me. I'm supposed to be sent to London on business any day now."
"I'm not a lawyer, dear fellow... So, wait two years and marry her."
"I'm married, Professor!"
"Ah, gentlemen, gentlemen!"
Doors opened, faces changed, instruments clattered in the cupboard, and Filipp Filippovich worked without stop.
"A vile apartment," the dog thought, "but how good it is here! What the hell did he need me for? Is he really going to let me live? What a weirdo! A single wink from him and he'd get such a fine dog it would take your breath away! Maybe I'm handsome too. It's my good luck! But the owl is garbage. Arrogant."
The dog woke up at last late in the evening, when the bells stopped and just at the instant when the door let in special visitors. There were four at once. All young people, and all dressed very modestly.
"What do these want?" the dog thought with surprise. Filipp Filippovich greeted them with much greater hostility. He stood at his desk and regarded them like a general looking at the enemy. The nostrils of his aquiline nose flared. The arrivals shuffled their feet on the carpet.
"We are here, Professor," said the one with a topknot of about a half foot of thick, curly black hair, "on this matter—"
"Gentlemen, you shouldn't go around without galoshes in this weather," Filipp Filippovich interrupted edifyingly. "First, you will catch cold, and second, you've left tracks on my carpets, and all my carpets are Persian."
The one with the topknot shut up and all four stared in astonishment at Filipp Filippovich. The silence extended to several seconds and it was broken by Filipp Filippovich's fingers drumming on the painted wooden plate on his desk.
"First of all, we're not gentlemen," said the youngest of the four, who had a peachy look.
"First of all," interrupting him as well, Filipp Filippovich asked, "are you a man or a woman?"
The four shut up and gaped once again. This time the first one, with the hair, responded. "What difference does it make, Comrade?" he asked haughtily.

"I'm a woman," admitted the peachy youth in the leather jacket and blushed mightily. After him, one of the other arrivals, a blond man in a tall fur hat, blushed dark red for some reason.
"In that case, you may keep your cap on; but you, gracious sir, I ask to remove your headgear," Filipp Filippovich said imposingly.
"I'm not your 'gracious sir'," the blond youth muttered in embarrassment, removing his hat.
"We have come to you—" the dark-haired one began again.
"First of all, who is this 'we'?"
"We are the new managing board of our building," the dark one said with contained fury. "I am Shvonder, she is Vyazemskaya, he is Comrade Pestrukhin, and Sharovkin. And so we—"
"You're the ones who have been moved into the apartment of Fyodor Pavlovich Sablin?"
"We are," Shvonder replied.
"God! The Kalabukhov house is doomed!" Filipp Filippovich exclaimed in despair and threw his hands up in the air.
"What are you laughing about, Professor?"
"I'm not laughing! I'm in complete despair!" shouted Filipp Filippovich. "What will happen to the central heating now?"
"You are mocking us, Professor Preobrazhensky!"
"What business brings you here? Make it fast, I'm on my way to dinner."
"We, the Building Committee," Shvonder said with hatred, "have come to you after the general meeting of the residents of our building, on the agenda of which was the question of consolidating the apartments."
"Where was this agenda?" screamed Filipp Filippovich. "Make an effort to express your ideas more clearly."
"The question of consolidating—"
"Enough! I understand! You know that by the resolution of 12th August of this year my apartment is exempt from all and any consolidation and resettlement?"
"We know," Shvonder replied, "but the general meeting examined your case and came to the conclusion that in particular and on the whole you occupy an excessive space. Completely excessive. You live alone in seven rooms."
"I live and work alone in seven rooms," replied Filipp Filippovich, "and I would like to have an eighth. I need it as a library."
The foursome froze.

"An eighth! Ho-ho-ho," said the blond man deprived of his headgear, "that's really something!"
"It's indescribable!" explained the youth who turned out to be a girl.
"I have a reception—note that it is also the library—a dining room and my study—that's three. Examining room, four. Operating room, five. My bedroom makes six, and the maids' room is seven. Basically, it's not enough... But that's not important. My apartment is exempt and that's the end of the conversation. May I go to dinner?"
"Sorry," said the fourth, who looked like a sturdy beetle.
"Sorry," Shvonder interrupted, "it is precisely the dining room and examining room that we came to discuss. The general meeting asks you voluntarily, as part of labour discipline, to give up the dining room. No one has dining rooms in Moscow anymore."
"Not even Isadora Duncan!"* the woman cried out resoundingly.
Something happened to Filipp Filippovich, the consequence of which was a gentle reddening of the face, but he did not utter a sound, waiting for what would come next.
"And the examining room too," Shvonder continued. "The examining room can easily be combined with the study."
"Ah-ha," said Filipp Filippovich in a strange voice. "And where am I supposed to partake of meals?"
"In the bedroom," all four chorused.
Filipp Filippovich's crimson colour took on a greyish cast.
"Take food in the bedroom," he said in a slightly stifled voice, "read in the examining room, dress in the reception room, operate in the maid's room, and examine people in the dining room? It's quite possible that Isadora Duncan does just that. Maybe she dines in the study and cuts up rabbits in the bathroom. Perhaps. But I am not Isadora Duncan!" he burst out, and his purple colour turned yellow. "I will eat in the dining room and operate in the operating room! Tell this to the general meeting, and I entreat you humbly to return to your affairs and allow me to take food where all normal people do—that is, in the dining room, and not in the entrance and not in the nursery."
"Then, Professor, in view of your stubborn resistance," said agitated Shvonder, "we will file a complaint against you higher up."
"Aha," Filipp Filippovich said, "is that so?" His voice took on a suspiciously polite tone. "I'll ask you to wait a minute."
"That's some guy," thought the dog delightedly. "Just like me. Oh, he's going to nip them now, oh, he will! I don't know how yet, but he'll nip them!... Hit them! Take that long-legged one right above the boot on his knee tendon... Grrrrr."

Filipp Filippovich picked up the telephone receiver with a bang and said this into it: "Please... yes... thank you. Vitaly Alexandrovich, please. Professor Preobrazhensky. Vitaly Alexandrovich? Very glad to find you in. Thank you, I'm fine. Vitaly Alexandrovich, your operation is being cancelled. What? No, cancelled completely, just like all the other operations. Here is why: I am stopping work in Moscow and in Russia in general... Four people just came in to see me, one of them is a woman dressed as a man and two are armed with revolvers, and they terrorized me in my apartment with the goal of taking part of it away—"

"Excuse me, Professor," Shvonder began, his expression changed.

"Sorry... I do not have the opportunity to repeat everything they said, I'm not interested in nonsense. It is enough to say that they proposed I give up my examining room, in other words, making it necessary to operate on you where I have been slaughtering rabbits until now. In such conditions I not only cannot work but I do not have the right to work. Therefore, I am ending my activity, closing up the apartment, and moving to Sochi. I can turn over the keys to Shvonder, let him perform the operations."

The foursome froze. Snow melted on their boots.

"What else can I do?... I'm very unhappy about it myself... What? Oh, no, Vitaly Alexandrovich! Oh no! I will not continue this way. My patience has run out. This is the second time since August. What? Hm... As you wish. But at least... But only on this condition: from whomever, whenever, whatever, but it must be a paper that will keep Shvonder and everyone else from even approaching the door to my apartment. A final paper. Factual. Real. A seal. So that my name is not even mentioned. Of course. I am dead to them. Yes, yes. Please. Who? Aha... Well, that's better. Aha. All right. I'll pass the phone over. Please be so kind," Filipp Filippovich said in a snake-like voice, "someone wants to speak to you."

"Excuse me, Professor," Shvonder said, flaring up and then fading, "you perverted our words."

"I will ask you not to use such expressions."

Shvonder distractedly took the receiver and said, "I'm listening. Yes... chairman of the BuildCom... We were acting in accordance with the rules... the professor is in a completely exceptional situation as it is... We know about his work... we were going to leave an entire five rooms... well, all right... if that's the case... all right..."

Completely red, he hung up and turned.

"He really showed him! What a guy!" the dog thought in delight. "Does he know some special word? You can beat me all you like now, but I'm not ever leaving here!"
Three of them, mouths agape, stared at the humiliated Shvonder.
"This is shameful," he muttered diffidently.
"If we were to have a discussion now," the woman began, excited and with flaming cheeks, "I would prove to Vitaly Alexandrovich..."
"Forgive me, you're not planning to open the discussion this minute, are you?" Filipp Filippovich asked politely.
The woman's eyes burned.
"I understand your irony, Professor, we will be leaving... Only... As chairman of the cultural section of the building "
"Chair-wo-man," Filipp Filippovich corrected.
"I want to ask you," and here the woman pulled out several bright and snow-sodden magazines from inside her coat, "to buy a few magazines to help the children of France. Half a rouble each."
"No, I won't," Filipp Filippovich replied brusquely, squinting at the magazines.
Total astonishment showed on their faces, and the woman's complexion took on a cranberry hue.
"Why are you refusing?"
"I don't want to."
"Don't you feel sympathy for the children of France?"
"I do."
"Do you begrudge the fifty copecks?"
"No."
"Then why?"
"I don't want to."
A silence ensued.
"You know, Professor," said the girl after a deep sigh, "If you weren't a European luminary and you weren't protected in the most outrageous manner (the blond man tugged at the hem of her jacket, but she waved him off) by people whom, I am certain, we will discover, you should be arrested!"
"For what exactly?" Filipp Filippovich asked with curiosity.
"You hate the proletariat!" the woman said hotly.
"Yes, I don't like the proletariat," Filipp Filippovich agreed sadly and pressed a button. A bell rang somewhere. The door to the hallway opened.
"Zina," Filipp Filippovich shouted. "Serve dinner. Do you mind, gentlemen?"

The foursome silently left the study, silently went through the reception, silently through the entrance, and behind them came the sound of the front door shutting heavily and resoundingly.
The dog stood on his hind legs and performed a kind of prayer dance before Filipp Filippovich.

Chapter 3

The dishes, painted with paradisaical flowers and a wide black rim, held thin slices of salmon and marinated eel. On the heavy board was a chunk of sweating cheese, and in a silver bowl, surrounded by snow, was caviar. Among the plates stood several slender shot glasses and three crystal decanters with vodkas of different colours. All these objects resided on a small marble table cosily nestled up against the enormous carved oak sideboard, erupting with bursts of glass and silver light. In the centre of the room stood a table, as heavy as a gravestone, under a white cloth, and on it were two settings, napkins folded into bishops' mitres and three dark bottles.

Zina brought in a covered silver dish with something grumbling inside. The fragrance coming from the dish made the dog's mouth fill with watery saliva instantly. "The Gardens of Semiramide!"* he thought and started banging his tail like a stick on the parquet floor.

"Bring them here!" Filipp Filippovich commanded with the air of a predator. "Doctor Bormental, I tell you, leave the caviar be! If you would like to take some good advice, have the ordinary Russian vodka, not the English."

The handsome bitten one (he was no longer wearing the lab coat but was in a decent black suit) shrugged his broad shoulders, chuckled politely, and poured himself the clear vodka.

"The newly blessed?"* he enquired.

"Bless you, dear fellow," the host replied. "It's spirit alcohol. Darya Petrovna makes excellent vodka herself."

"You know, Filipp Filippovich, everyone says that it's quite decent now. Sixty proof."

"But vodka must be eighty proof, not sixty, first of all," Filipp Filippovich interrupted with a lecture. "And secondly, God only knows what they may have added to it. Can you predict what they could come up with?"

"Anything at all," the bitten one said confidently.

"I am of the same opinion," added Filipp Filippovich and tossed the contents of his glass as a single lump into his throat. "Eh... Mmm... Doctor Bormental, I entreat you: take this thing instantly, and if you say it's not... then I will be your mortal enemy for life. 'From Seville to Granada...'"

With those words, he hooked something resembling a small dark loaf of bread on his palmate silver fork. The bitten one followed his example. Filipp Filippovich's eyes glowed.

"Is this bad?" Filipp Filippovich asked, chewing. "Is it? You tell me, esteemed doctor."

"It's exquisite," the bitten one replied sincerely.

"Of course... Please note, Ivan Arnoldovich, that only the remaining landowners not yet slaughtered by the Bolsheviks use cold hors d'oeuvres or soup as *zakuski* for vodka.* Any even slightly self-respecting person operates with hot *zakuski*. And of the hot *zakuski* of Moscow, this is number one. They used to be prepared marvellously once upon a time at the Slavyansky Bazaar. Here!"

"You're giving the dog food from the table," a woman's voice sounded, "and then you won't be able to lure him out of here with a fresh-baked round loaf."

"It's all right. The poor thing was starved." Filipp Filippovich used his fork to serve the dog the titbit, which was accepted with prestidigitatorial agility, and then tossed the fork with a clatter into the rinse bowl.

Next, steam redolent of crayfish rose from the plates; the dog sat in the shade of the tablecloth with the air of a watchman at a gunpowder warehouse, while Filipp Filippovich tucked the tail of the taut napkin into his collar and preached: "Food, Ivan Arnoldovich, is a tricky thing. One must know how to eat, and just imagine, the majority of people don't know how at all. One needs to know not only what to eat but when and how." (Filipp Filippovich waved his spoon significantly.) "And what to say, yes! If you care about your digestion, here is good advice—do not talk about Bolshevism or medicine while eating. And, God forbid, don't read Soviet newspapers before dinner!"

"Hm... But there are no others."

"So don't read any. You know, I did thirty observations at my clinic. And what do you think? The patients who did not read newspapers felt wonderful. The ones I had read *Pravda* lost weight!"

"Hm?" the bitten one responded with interest, turning pink with soup and wine.

"Moreover, reduced knee reflexes, poor appetite and depression."

"The Devil!..."

"Yes. But what am I doing? I brought up medicine myself. Let's eat instead."

Filipp Filippovich leant back, rang, and Zina appeared in the cherry-wood doorway. The dog was given a pale and fat piece of sturgeon, which he didn't like, and immediately after it a piece of rare roast beef. Gobbling it down, the dog suddenly realized that he was sleepy and couldn't look at any more food. "A strange sensation," he thought, shutting his heavy lids, "my eyes don't want to see any food. And smoking after dinner is stupid."

The dining room filled with unpleasant blue cigar smoke. The dog dozed, head on top of his front paws.

"Saint-Julien is a decent wine," the dog heard in his sleep, "but you can't get it any more."

A soft chorale, dampened by ceilings and carpets, reached them from above and the side.

Filipp Filippovich rang, and Zina entered.

"Zinusha, what does this mean?"

"They're having a general meeting again, Filipp Filippovich," Zina replied.

"Again!" Filipp Filippovich cried bitterly. "Well, that's the beginning of the end! The Kalabukhov house is doomed! I'll have to move, but where, I ask you? It's a slippery slope. First there will be singing every night, then the pipes will freeze in the toilets, then the boiler will burst in the central heating system, and so on. It's curtains for Kalabukhov!"

"Filipp Filippovich is grieving," Zina noted with a smile and carried away a mound of dishes.

"How could I not grieve?" howled Filipp Filippovich. "What a building this was! You must understand!"

"You take too grim a view of things, Filipp Filippovich," countered the handsome bitten one. "They have changed acutely now."

"Dear fellow, you know me! Right? I am a man of facts, a man of observation. I am an enemy of unsubstantiated hypotheses. And that is very well known not only in Russia but in Europe. If I say something, that means it is based on a fact from which I draw my conclusion. And here is a fact for you: the coat rack and galoshes stand in our building."

"Interesting..."

"Galoshes—that's nonsense, happiness does not lie in galoshes," thought the dog, "but he's an outstanding character."

"Let me put it to you—the galoshes stand. I have lived in this building since 1903. And throughout that time until April 1917 there has not been a single incident—and I underline 'not a single' in red pencil!—of even one pair of galoshes disappearing from our lobby downstairs, with the front door never locked. Note that there are twelve apartments here and I have visiting hours. In April 1917, one fine day all the galoshes disappeared, including two pairs belonging to me, three walking sticks, an overcoat and the doorman's samovar. Ever since then the galoshes stand ceased to exist. My dear fellow! I'm not talking about the central heating! I'm not! Let it be. If we're in a social revolution, there shouldn't be heating! Though someday, if I have the free time, I'll study the brain and prove that all this social twaddle is nothing but delirium... So I say: why, when this whole business began, did everyone start walking in dirty galoshes and felt boots on the marble stairs? Why must the galoshes still be locked up and have a soldier posted to keep them from being swiped? Why did they remove the carpeting from the main staircase? Does Karl Marx* forbid carpets on the stairs? Is it written anywhere in Karl Marx that the second entrance of the Kalabukhov house on Prechistenka must be boarded up and people have to go around through the back door? Who needs that? The oppressed Negroes? Or the Portuguese workers? Why can't the proletariat leave its galoshes downstairs instead of dirtying the marble?"

"But it doesn't even have any galoshes, Filipp Filippovich," the bitten one tried to say.

"Nothing of the sort!" Filipp Filippovich replied in thunderous tones and poured a glass of wine. "Hm... I don't approve of liqueurs after dinner, they weigh you down and have a deleterious effect on the liver... Nothing of the sort! The proletariat has galoshes, and those galoshes are mine! They are the very same galoshes that disappeared on 13th April 1917. I ask you, who swiped them? I? Impossible! The bourgeois Sablin?" (Filipp Filippovich pointed at the ceiling.) "Ridiculous to contemplate! The sugar-plant owner Polozov?" (Filipp Filippovich pointed to the side.) "Not in any case! It was done by those songsters! Yes! But why can't they take them off when they're on the stairs?" (Filipp Filippovich was turning purple.) "Why the hell did they remove the flowers from the landings? Why does the electricity, which—God help my memory here—went out twice in twenty years, now dim every single month? Doctor Bormental! Statistics are a cruel thing. You, who are familiar with my latest work, know this better than anyone!"

"It's the ruination, Filipp Filippovich!"

"No," Filipp Filippovich countered with complete confidence, "no, it's not. You be the first, dear Ivan Arnoldovich, to refrain from using that word. It's a mirage, smoke, fiction!" Filipp Filippovich spread his stubby fingers, making two shadows resembling tortoises wriggle on the tablecloth. "What is this ruination of yours? An old hag with a crutch?* A witch who smashed out all the window glass and put out all the lamps? She simply doesn't exist. What do you mean by that word?" Filipp Filippovich demanded angrily from the poor cardboard duck hanging upside down near the buffet, and answered for it. "Here's what it is: if I, instead of operating every evening, start singing in chorus in my apartment, ruination will befall me! If I start, forgive me for saying this, start missing the toilet bowl when I piss, and so do Zina and Darya Petrovna, there will be ruination in the toilet. Therefore, ruination is not in the toilets, it's in people's heads! That means, when those baritones shout 'Beat the ruination!' I laugh." (Filipp Filippovich's face contorted so much that the bitten one gaped.) "I swear, it makes me laugh! It means that every one of them should smack himself on the head! And then, when he beats the world revolution, Engels and Nikolai Romanov,* the oppressed Malayans and other such hallucinations out of his head and starts cleaning out the sheds—his actual job—the ruin will vanish on its own. You cannot serve two gods at once! It is impossible simultaneously to sweep the trolley tracks and save some Spanish beggars! No one can manage that, Doctor, and especially not people who are already two hundred years behind the Europeans in development and still can't button their own trousers very effectively!"

Filipp Filippovich had fallen into a rage. His hawk-like nostrils flared. Strengthened by his full dinner, he thundered like an ancient prophet, and his head sparked silver.

His words fell on the sleepy dog like a quiet underground buzz. Sometimes the owl with the stupid yellow eyes flashed in his dreamy visions; then the vile mug of the executioner in the dirty white cap; then Filipp Filippovich's cavalier's moustache, lit by the harsh electricity from the lampshade; then sleepy sleighs creaked and vanished, while the ravaged piece of roast beef cooked in juices in the dog's stomach.

"He could earn money at rallies," the dog dreamt woozily, "a first-class businessman. Of course, he doesn't seem to be short of funds as it is..."

"Police!" shouted Filipp Filippovich. "Police!"

"Glug-glug-glug!" Bubbles burst in the dog's brain.

"Police! That, and only that! It matters not at all whether he has a badge or a red kepi. Put a policeman next to every person and force that policeman to moderate the vocal outbursts of our citizens. You say, ruination! I will tell you, Doctor, that nothing will change for the better in our building, or in any other building, until you quieten those singers! As soon as they stop their concerts, the situation will improve on its own!"

"You are making counter-revolutionary statements, Filipp Filippovich," joked the bitten one. "Pray God no one hears you!"

"Nothing dangerous!" Filipp Filippovich retorted heatedly. "No counter-revolution! By the way, there's another word I absolutely can't stand! There's no way of knowing what's hidden by it! The Devil only knows! So I say: there is nothing counter-revolutionary in my words. There is only common sense and life experience."

Here Filipp Filippovich moved the tail of the shiny, cracked napkin from his collar, crumpled it up and laid it next to the unfinished glass of red wine. The bitten one immediately stood and thanked him: "*Merci*."

"Just a minute, Doctor!" Filipp Filippovich stopped him and took out his wallet from his pocket. He squinted, counted out white notes and handed them to the bitten one with the words, "Today, you are owed forty roubles, Ivan Arnoldovich. Here you are!"

The man who suffered the dog bite thanked him and, blushing, stuffed the money into his jacket pocket.

"Will you be needing me this evening, Filipp Filippovich?" he enquired.

"No, thank you, dear fellow. We won't be doing anything today. First of all, the rabbit died, and secondly, they're doing *Aida* at the Bolshoi. I haven't heard it in a long time. I love it... Remember the duet?... Tara... ra-rim..."

"How do you find time for everything, Filipp Filippovich?" the doctor asked respectfully.

"He who never hurries always arrives everywhere on time," explained his host. "Of course, if I were to jump around to various meetings and warble like a nightingale all day instead of doing my actual work, I wouldn't have time to go anywhere." Filipp Filippovich's fingers pressed the button on his watch and the heavenly chimes played in his pocket. "Just after eight... I'll get there for the second act... I am a believer in the division of labour. Let them sing at the Bolshoi, and I'll do surgery. That's fine—and no ruination... Now, Ivan Arnoldovich, keep an eye out: as soon as there is a suitable death, straight from the table into a nutrient liquid and bring it to me!"

"Don't worry, Filipp Filippovich, the pathology anatomists have promised me."

"Excellent, and in the meantime we'll observe this street neurasthenic, give him a good wash. Let his side heal."

"He's concerned about me," thought the dog. "A very good man. I know who he is! He is a good wizard, a witch and magician from a canine fairy tale... This can't be just a dream, can it? What if it is?" (The dog shuddered in his sleep.) "I'll wake up and there won't be anything here. No lamp in silks, no warmth, no satiety. Back to the alley, horrible blizzard, icy asphalt, hunger, mean people... The cafeteria, the snow... God, how hard that will be!"

Chapter 4

But none of that happened. It was the alley that melted like a bad dream and did not return.

You could see that the ruination was not so terrible! Despite it, twice a day the grey accordions under the window sill filled with heat, and warmth spread in waves throughout the apartment.

It was perfectly clear: the dog had got the top prize ticket in the canine lottery. His eyes now filled with grateful tears addressed to the wise man of Prechistenka at least twice a day. Besides which, all the cheval glass in the living room, in the reception area between the wardrobes reflected the lucky and handsome dog.

"I am handsome. Perhaps an unknown canine prince incognito," pondered the dog, looking at the shaggy coffee-coloured dog with a satisfied mug strolling in the mirrored distance. "It's quite possible that my grandmother had a fling with a Newfoundland. I see that there is a white spot on my face. Where did it come from, you may ask? Filipp Filippovich is a man of great taste and he wouldn't pick up any old stray dog he came across."

In the course of a week, the dog ate as much as he had in the last six hungry weeks on the streets. But that was only in terms of weight. There was no need to talk about the quality of the food at Filipp Filippovich's. Even if you don't count the mountain of scraps Darya Petrovna bought every day at the market for eighteen copecks, it's enough to mention the dinners at 7 p.m. in the dining room, which the dog attended, despite the protests of the graceful Zina. During these dinners, Filipp Filippovich completely attained the calling of divinity. The dog stood on his hind legs and chewed his jacket... the dog learnt Filipp Filippovich's ring—two full-voiced bursts of the master's push—and flew out barking to greet him in the entrance. The master strode in wearing the dark-brown fox, glistening with a million snowflakes, smelling of tangerines, cigars, perfume, lemons, petrol, eau de cologne, cloth, and his voice, like a commanding trumpet, carried throughout the residence:

"You pig, why did you tear apart the owl? Was it bothering you? Was it, I ask you? Why did you break Professor Mechnikov?"*

"He needs to be whipped, Filipp Filippovich, at least once," Zina said in outrage, "or he'll be thoroughly spoilt. Just look what he did to your galoshes!"

"No one should be whipped," Filipp Filippovich said agitatedly, "remember that once and for all! Humans and animals can be influenced only by suggestion! Did you give him meat today?"
"Lord! He's eaten us out of house and home! How can you ask, Filipp Filippovich? I'm amazed that he doesn't burst!"
"Let him eat to his heart's content!... How did the owl bother you, you hooligan?"
"Oooo-ooo," whined the toadying dog, crawling on his belly, legs twisted out.
Then he was dragged by the scruff of his neck through the reception to the study with great hue and cry. The dog howled, snapped, clawed at the rug and rode on his backside, like in the circus.
In the middle of the study on the rug lay the glass-eyed owl, its torn belly spilling red rags smelling of camphor. A shattered portrait's smithereens were scattered on the desk.
"I left it like this on purpose so that you could enjoy the sight," an upset Zina reported. "He jumped up on the desk, what a scoundrel! And grabbed the owl by the tail, snap! He tore it up before I caught my breath! Rub his nose in the owl, Filipp Filippovich, so he knows not to ruin things!"
And the howling began. They dragged the dog, glued to the rug, to rub his nose in the owl, while the dog wept bitter tears and thought, "Beat me, just don't chase me from the apartment."
"Send the owl to the taxidermist today. Besides that, here is eight roubles plus fifteen copecks for the tram, go to Muir's* and buy him a good collar with a chain."
The next day they put a wide, shiny collar on the dog. At first, when he looked in the mirror, he was very upset, tucked in his tail and went to the bathroom, wondering how to tear it off against a trunk or a box. But very quickly the dog realized that he was a fool. Zina took him for a walk on the chain. On Obukhov Lane the dog walked like a prisoner, burning with shame, but having walked along Prechistenka to the Church of Christ the Saviour, he realized full well what a collar means in life. Wild envy burned in the eyes of every dog they encountered, and near Myortvy Lane some long-limbed stray with a bobbed tail barked and cursed him as aristocratic scum and a suck-up. When they crossed the trolley tracks, the policeman regarded his collar with pleasure and respect, and when they returned, the most amazing thing in his life occurred: Fyodor the doorman personally unlocked the front door and let in Sharik, saying to Zina: "What a shaggy dog Filipp Filippovich has! And astonishingly fat."

"And how! He eats for six!" explained Zina, made rosy and beautiful by the frost.
"A collar is like a briefcase," thought the dog wittily and, wagging his behind, sashayed up to the second floor like an aristocrat.
Now appreciating the collar's value, the dog made his first visit to the main department of paradise, from which he had been categorically banned until now, to wit—the kingdom of the cook, Darya Petrovna. The entire apartment wasn't worth two bits of Darya's kingdom. Every day, flames sparked and roared in the stove, black on top and tiled. The stove crackled. Darya Petrovna's face burned with eternally fiery torment and unquenched passion in the crimson columns. It shone and glistened with fat. Twenty-two artificial diamonds glowed in her fashionably done light hair, combed over her ears and caught in a bun at the nape. Golden pots hung from hooks on the walls, the entire kitchen was a racket of smells, gurgling and hissing in closed vessels...
"Out!" shrieked Darya Petrovna. "Out, you homeless pickpocket! You're the last thing I need in here! I'll take the poker to you—"
"Now, now... Why are you barking at me?" the dog squinted sweetly. "I'm no pickpocket! Can't you see my collar?" He pushed at the door with his side, poking his nose through it.
Sharik the dog had some secret in conquering people's hearts. Two days later he was lying next to the coal basket and watching Darya Petrovna work. She used a sharp narrow knife to chop off the heads and feet of helpless grouse and then like a furious executioner she tore flesh from the bones, pulled entrails out of the hens and twirled something in the meat grinder. At the same time, Sharik tore at a grouse head. Darya Petrovna pulled out pieces of soaked bread from a bowl of milk, mixed them with the ground meat on a board, poured cream over it all, salted it and shaped patties on the same board. The burner roared as if there was a house fire, and inside the skillet things burbled, bubbled and skittered. The damper leapt up with a clang revealing a horrible hell. Spurting, gushing...
In the evening, the stone jaws went dim, and the dark and important Prechistenka night with its lone star showed in the kitchen window above the white half-curtain. In the kitchen, the floor was damp, the pots glowed mysteriously and dully, and a fireman's cap lay on the table. Sharik lay on the warm stove like a lion on the gates and, one ear cocked in curiosity, watched the black-moustachioed and excited man wearing a broad leather belt behind the half-shut door to Zina and Darya Petrovna's room embrace Darya Petrovna. Her face burned with torment and passion, all of it except her cadaverous powdered nose. A

crack of light lay on a picture of the black-moustachioed man, and an Easter rose hung down from it.

"You're as persistent as a demon," Darya Petrovna muttered in the semi-darkness. "Stop it. Zina will be back any minute. Really, did you get the rejuvenation treatment too?"

"We don't need it," the man with the black moustache replied in a husky voice, barely able to control himself. "You are so fiery..."

In the evenings, the Prechistenka star was hidden behind heavy drapes, and if there was no performance of *Aida* at the Bolshoi and there was no meeting of the All-Russian Surgical Society, the god settled into an armchair. There were no lights on the ceiling, and only a single green lamp burned on the desk. Sharik lay on the carpet in the shadows and stared at the horrible business. Human brains lay in a disgustingly toxic and murky liquid in glass jars. The god's hands, bare to the elbow, were covered in reddish rubber gloves, and his slippery dull fingers rummaged in the grooves. Sometimes the god armed himself with a small glinting knife and quietly cut the firm yellow brains.

"To the sacred banks of the Nile,"* sang the god softly, biting his lips and recalling the golden interior of the Bolshoi Theatre.

The pipes were heated to the highest point at that hour. Their warmth rose to the ceiling, spreading from there throughout the room, and in the dog's fur the last flea, as yet not combed out by Filipp Filippovich but already doomed, grew animated. And then the front door shut in the distance.

"Zinka's off to the cinema," thought the dog. "And when she returns, we'll have supper. I think there will be veal cutlets for supper."

On that terrible day, in the morning, Sharik was pricked by a premonition. As a result he suddenly grew morose and ate breakfast—half a cup of oatmeal and yesterday's lamb bone—without any appetite. He moped to the reception and howled lightly at his own reflection. But after Zina took him for a walk on the boulevard, the day went normally. There were no office hours today, because, as you know, there are no office hours on Tuesdays, and the god sat in the study, some heavy books with bright pictures spread on his desk. They waited for lunch. The dog perked up at the thought that the third dish today, as he had definitely learnt in the kitchen, would be turkey. Walking down the corridor, the dog heard the telephone ring unpleasantly and unexpectedly in Filipp Filippovich's study. Filipp Filippovich answered, listened and suddenly grew agitated.

"Excellent," said his voice, "bring him right away, immediately!"

He moved about, rang, and told Zina when she came in to serve lunch quickly. Lunch! Lunch! Lunch! Dishes clattered in the dining room. Zina started rushing about; Darya Petrovna could be heard grumbling in the kitchen that the turkey wasn't done.

The dog grew worried again.

"I don't like a hubbub in the apartment," he thought. No sooner had he thought it than the hubbub took on an even more unpleasant character. Primarily due to the appearance of Doctor Bormental, whom he had once bitten. He brought a bad-smelling suitcase and, without even taking off his coat, rushed off with it down the corridor to the examining room. Filipp Filippovich dropped his unfinished cup of coffee, which never happened, and ran to meet Bormental, which never happened with him either.

"When did he die?" he shouted.

"Three hours ago," Bormental replied, opening the suitcase without removing his snow-covered hat.

"Who died?" thought the dog grumpily and unhappily, getting underfoot. "I can't stand it when people bustle around."

"Get out of the way! Hurry, hurry, hurry!" shouted Filipp Filippovich in all directions and rang all the bells, as it seemed to the dog.

Zina ran in.

"Zina! Put Darya Petrovna on the phone, to write down all calls, let no one come! I need you. Doctor Bormental, I implore you, hurry, hurry!"

"I don't like this, I don't," the dog frowned in offence and wandered around the apartment, while all the bustle was concentrated in the examining room. Zina appeared suddenly in a white coat resembling a shroud and ran back and forth between the examining room and the kitchen.

"Should I get some grub? The hell with them," decided the dog and got a sudden surprise.

"Don't give Sharik anything!" thundered the command from the examining room.

"Like I can keep an eye on him!"

"Lock him up!"

Sharik was lured and locked in the bathroom.

"Rudeness," thought Sharik, sitting in the dim bathroom, "utter stupidity..."

He spent almost quarter of an hour in the bathroom in a strange mood—sometimes angry, sometimes deeply depressed. Everything was dreary and unclear... "Fine, you'll have yourself galoshes tomorrow, my esteemed Filipp Filippovich," he thought. "You've already had to buy two pairs, now you'll buy another. Teach you to lock up dogs."

But suddenly his furious thought was interrupted. Unexpectedly and clearly he recalled a piece of his earliest youth, the sunny huge expanse of the courtyard near the Preobrazhenskaya Gate, the shards of sunshine in bottles, the broken brick, the free stray dogs...

"No, no way can I leave here to be free, why lie," said the dog drearily, breathing through his nose, "I'm used to it. I'm a gentleman's dog, an intelligent creature; I've tasted a better life. And what is freedom anyway? Just smoke, a mirage, a fiction... The delirium of those miserable democrats..."

Then the dimness in the bathroom became terrible; he howled, threw himself against the door, began scratching at it.

"Ooo-ooo-ooo!" The sound travelled through the apartment as if in a barrel.

"I'll tear up the owl again!" the dog thought wildly, but impotently. Then he weakened, lay still, and when he stood up again, his hackles rose: for some reason he imagined the disgusting eyes of a wolf in the bath...

At the peak of his torment, the door opened. The dog came out, shook himself, and gloomily headed for the kitchen, but Zina firmly led him by the collar to the examining room. A chill shot below the dog's heart.

"What do they need me for?" he thought suspiciously. "My side has healed. I don't understand."

And his paws slid over the slippery parquet floor, and that's how he was delivered to the examining room. He was struck right away by the unusual lighting. The white globe on the ceiling glowed so much that it hurt his eyes. In the white radiance stood a priest, softly singing about the sacred banks of the Nile. Only a vague scent let him recognize Filipp Filippovich. His trimmed grey hair was hidden under a white cap that resembled a patriarch's skullcap. The priest was all in white, and over the white, like a scapular, was a narrow rubber apron. His hands were in black gloves.

The bitten one was also wearing a skullcap. The long table was unfolded, and a small square one on a shiny leg had been moved next to it.

Here the dog began to hate the bitten one more than anything, and mostly because of his eyes today. Usually bold and direct, now they ran in all directions away from the dog's eyes. They were tense, false, and in their depths was hidden a bad, nasty deed, if not an entire

crime. The dog gave him a heavy, troubled look and went into the corner.
"The collar, Zina," Filipp Filippovich said softly. "Just don't excite him."
Zina's eyes instantly became just as vile as the bitten one's. She came over to the dog and petted him with blatant falseness. He gave her a sad and scornful look.
"Well, there's three of you. You'll get me if you want. But you're ashamed... If I only knew what you're going to do with me."
Zina undid his collar, the dog shook his head and snorted. The bitten one arose before him with a vile, dizzying odour coming from him.
"Pfui, disgusting... Why do I feel so dizzy and afraid?" thought the dog and backed away from the bitten one.
"Hurry, Doctor," Filipp Filippovich said impatiently.
There was a sharp, sweet smell in the air. The bitten one, never taking his wary, lousy eyes from the dog, took his right hand from behind his back and quickly poked the dog's nose with a wad of damp cotton. Sharik was stunned, his head spun lightly, but he managed to back away. The bitten one leapt after him and suddenly plastered his face with the cotton. His breathing was blocked, but the dog managed to struggle free once more. "Villain," flashed through his mind. "What for?" They plastered his nose again. Suddenly, in the middle of the examining room a lake appeared with very cheery spectral pink dogs in rowing boats on it. His legs lost their bones and bent.
"On the table!" Filipp Filippovich's words crashed somewhere in a merry voice and dissolved in orange streams. The horror vanished, replaced by joy, and for about two seconds the fading dog loved the bitten one. Then the whole world turned upside down and he still felt a cold but pleasant hand under his belly. Then—nothing.
The dog Sharik lay splayed on the narrow operating table, and his head beat helplessly on the white oilcloth pillow. His stomach was shaved and now Doctor Bormental, panting and hurrying, shaved Sharik's head with a machine, digging into the fur. Filipp Filippovich, leaning his hands on the edge of the table, watched the procedure with his eyes as shiny as the gold frames of his glasses, and spoke in agitation:
"Ivan Arnoldovich, the most important moment is when I enter the *sella turcica*.* Instantly, I implore you, hand me the appendage and sew immediately! If it starts haemorrhaging there, we'll lose time and we'll lose the dog. Actually, there's no chance for him anyway." He paused, squinting one eye, and glanced, mockingly it seemed, into the

half-open sleeping eye of the dog, adding, "You know, I'm sorry for him. Just imagine, I'd grown used to him."
He waved his hands as he spoke, as if blessing the miserable dog Sharik before his difficult exploit. He was trying to keep any dust from landing on the black rubber.
The whitish skin of the dog glimmered beneath the shaved fur. Bormental tossed away the machine and armed himself with a razor. He soaped up the small, helpless head and started shaving. There was a strong crackling coming from the blade, and blood appeared in spots. Having finished shaving the head, the bitten one wiped it with a wet benzene rag, then stretched out the dog's naked belly, blew air out of his lips and said, "Ready."
Zina turned on the water in the sink and Bormental rushed to wash his hands. Zina poured alcohol over them from a vial.
"May I leave, Filipp Filippovich?" she asked, with a fearful look at the dog's shaved head.
"You may."
Zina vanished. Bormental bustled further. He tucked light gauze napkins all around Sharik's head, and then a never-seen bald canine skull and a strange bearded muzzle appeared on the pillow.
The priest moved. He straightened, looked at the dog's head, and said, "Well, bless us, Lord. Scalpel."
Bormental pulled out a small tubby knife from the sparkling pile on the little table and handed it to the priest. Then he donned black gloves just like the priest's.
"Is he asleep?" Filipp Filippovich asked.
"Fast asleep."
Filipp Filippovich's teeth clenched, his little eyes took on a sharp, spiky gleam and, raising up the scalpel, he drew a precise and long cut along Sharik's belly. The skin separated instantly, and blood spurted out in different directions. Bormental pounced like a predator, pressing on Sharik's wound with clumps of gauze, and then used small tweezers, like sugar tongs, to clamp its edges and it dried. Sweat broke out in bubbles on Bormental's brow.
Filipp Filippovich sliced a second time, and they both started tearing at Sharik's body with hooks, scissors and some sort of staples. Pink and yellow tissue, weeping with bloody dew, flew out. Filipp Filippovich twirled his knife in the body and then shouted, "Scissors!"
The instrument flashed in the bitten one's hands as if he were a magician. Filipp Filippovich dug deep and in a few turns tore out Sharik's testicles with some dangling bits from his body. Bormental,

completely wet with effort and excitement, rushed to a glass jar and removed other, wet and drooping testicles. Short damp strings leapt and twisted in the hands of the professor and assistant. Crooked needles clicked in the clamps, and the testicles were sewn in place of Sharik's. The priest fell back from the wound, poked it with a clump of gauze and ordered, "Sew up the skin instantly, Doctor!"
Then he looked over at the round white clock.
"We took fourteen minutes," Bormental said through clenched teeth, digging the crooked needle into the flabby skin.
Then both men grew more agitated, like murderers who were in a hurry.
"Scalpel!" shouted Filipp Filippovich.
The scalpel jumped into his hand as if by itself, after which Filipp Filippovich's face grew terrible. He bared his porcelain and gold crowns and in one stroke drew a bloody crown on Sharik's brow. They flipped over the skin with shorn hair like a scalp. They revealed the skull. Filipp Filippovich shouted, "Trepan!"
Bormental handed him the gleaming hand drill. Biting his lips, Filipp Filippovich began jabbing the instrument into the skull and drilling little holes a centimetre apart, so that they went all around the skull. He spent no more than five seconds per hole. Then using an unusual saw, sticking its tail into the first hole, he started sawing the way ladies' sewing kits are made. The skull buzzed and shook softly. In about three minutes they removed the top of Sharik's skull.
That revealed the dome of Sharik's brain, grey with bluish veins and reddish spots. Filipp Filippovich dug into the membranes with the scissors and opened them up. At one point, a thin fountain of blood gushed out, almost hitting the professor in the eye, spotting his cap. Bormental leapt like a tiger with artery forceps to staunch it and succeeded. Sweat slid in torrents from Bormental and his face turned meaty and multicoloured. His eyes raced from Filipp Filippovich's hands to the plate on the table. Filipp Filippovich had become positively terrifying. Hissing sounds came from his nose and his teeth were bared to the gums. He tore off the membrane from the brain and went deep inside, moving the hemispheres of the brain out of the opened bowl. At that moment Bormental went pale, grabbed Sharik's chest with one hand, and said hoarsely, "His pulse is falling rapidly."
Filipp Filippovich gave him a wild look, muttered something and dug in deeper. Bormental broke a glass ampoule with a crunch, sucked it into a hypodermic needle and treacherously injected Sharik somewhere near his heart.

"I'm headed for the *sella turcica*!" roared Filipp Filippovich and with his bloody, slippery gloves removed Sharik's yellow-grey brain from his head. For an instant he squinted at Sharik's muzzle, and Bormental immediately broke a second ampoule with yellow liquid and sucked it into a long hypodermic.
"Into the heart?" he asked meekly.
"Why are you still asking?" the professor roared angrily. "He's died on you five times by now. Inject! It's unthinkable!" His face had come to resemble an inspired highway robber.
The doctor took a swing and inserted the needle into the dog's heart.
"He's alive, just barely," he whispered meekly.
"There no time to discuss whether he's alive or not," fumed the terrible Filipp Filippovich, "I'm in the *sella*. He'll die anyway... Oh, damn... 'To the sacred banks...' Give me the appendage!"
Bormental handed him a jar in which a white lump dangled on a thread in liquid. "He has no equals in Europe, I swear," thought Bormental. With one hand, Filipp Filippovich pulled out the dangling lump, and with the other, using scissors, cut out a similar lump deep between the splayed hemispheres. He tossed Sharik's lump onto the plate and put the new one into the brain along with the thread and with his short fingers, which had miraculously become slender and flexible, managed to wrap it into place with the amber thread. After that he tossed out some clamps and forceps from Sharik's head, tucked the brain back into the brain pan, leant back and asked more calmly, "Dead, of course?"
"Thready pulse," replied Bormental.
"More adrenalin!"
The professor tossed the membrane over the brain, laid the sawn-off top neatly in place, moved the scalp back, and roared, "Sew!"
Bormental sewed up the head in about five minutes, breaking three needles.
And now on the pillow, a background coloured by blood, appeared Sharik's lifeless, dimmed muzzle with a ring wound around his head. Here Filipp Filippovich leant back completely, like a sated vampire, tore off one glove, shaking out a cloud of sweaty powder, tore a hole in the other, threw it on the floor and called, using the button on the wall.
Zina appeared in the doorway, head averted, so as not to see Sharik and the blood.
The priest removed the bloody skullcap with chalky hands and shouted, "Get me a cigarette right now, Zina. All fresh linens and a bath!"

He rested his chin on the edge of the table, opened the dog's right eye with two fingers, peered into the clearly dying eye and said, "There, damn it! He didn't die! Well, he will anyway. Ah, Doctor Bormental, I'm sorry about the dog! He was friendly, albeit wily."

Chapter 5

The notebook of Ivan Arnoldovich Bormental. A thin notebook the size of typing paper. Filled in Bormental's hand. The writing in the first two pages is neat, organized and clear; later, it becomes scrawled, agitated, with many blots.

22 December 1924. Monday.

CASE HISTORY

Laboratory dog approximately two years old. Male. Breed—mutt. Name—Sharik. Fur thin, in clumps, greyish brown with spots, tail the colour of baked milk. Traces of fully healed burn on left side. Nutrition before coming to the professor was poor; after a week's stay, very fat. Weight 8 kg (*exclamation mark*).

Heart, lungs, stomach, temperature within norm.

23 December. At 8.30 p.m. the first such operation in Europe developed by Professor Preobrazhensky was performed: under chloroform, Sharik's testicles were removed and replaced with a man's testicles with appendages and spermatic cords, taken from a 28-yr-old man who died 4 hours and 4 minutes before the operation and kept in sterile physiological liquid developed by Prof. Preobrazhensky.

Immediately thereafter, an appendage of the brain, the pituitary gland, was removed after trepanning the skull and replaced by a human one from the aforementioned man.

Introduced 8 cc of chloroform, 1 syringe of camphor, 2 syringes of adrenalin into the heart.

Reasons for the operation: an experiment by Preobrazhensky to combine transplantation of the pituitary gland and testicles to determine whether the pituitary gland is transplantable and, in the future, its influence on rejuvenation of humans.

Operation was performed by Prof. F.F. Preobrazhensky.

Assisted by Dr I.A. Bormental.

The night after the operation: threatening repeated drops in pulse. Expectation of fatal outcome. Huge doses of camphor per Preobrazhensky.

24 December. Morning—improvement. Respiratory rate doubled, temperature 42. Camphor and caffeine subcutaneously.

25 December. Deterioration of condition again. Pulse barely detected, cooling of extremities, no response in pupils. Adrenalin in the heart and camphor per Preobrazhensky, saline intravenously.

26 December. Some improvement. Pulse 180, respiration 92, temperature 41. Camphor, nutrition via enemas.
27 December. Pulse 152, breathing 50, temperature 39.8. Pupils respond. Camphor subcutaneously.
28 December. Significant improvement. At noon, a sudden drenching sweat. Temperature—37.0. Surgical wounds in previous condition. Re-bandaging. Appetite appeared. Liquid diet.
29 December. Sudden discovery of fur falling out on forehead and sides of body. Brought in for consultation: professor of Dermatology Faculty Vasily Vasilyevich Bundarev and the director of the Moscow Model Veterinary Institute. They consider the incident never described in the literature. Diagnosis remains unestablished. Temperature normal.
(Written in pencil:)
Tonight first bark (8.15). Noteworthy sharp change in timbre and tone (lower). Bark, instead of word "bow-wow", in syllable "a-o". In coloration, faintly resembles groaning.
30 December. Falling-out of fur has taken on the character of general balding. Weighing revealed unexpected result—weight is 30 kilos due to bone growth (lengthening). Dog still lying as before.
31 December. Colossal appetite.
(A splotch in the notebook. After the ink blot, in hasty scrawl:)
At 12.12 the dog clearly barked the word: "A-b-yr"!!
(There is a break in the notebook and then, apparently by mistake caused by agitation, it says):
1 December.
(Crossed out and corrected:)
1 January 1925. Photographed in the morning. Clearly barks "Abyr", repeating the word loudly and somehow joyfully. At 3 o'clock in the afternoon (*in capital letters*) he laughed, causing the maid Zina to faint. In the evening pronounced the word "Abyr-valg", "Abyr!" eight times in a row.
(In crooked letters written in pencil:)
The professor deciphered the word "Abyr-valg", it means "Glavryba", the fish store!!! Something monstr—
2 January. Photographed while smiling with magnesium flash.
Got out of bed and confidently stood for half an hour on his hind legs. Almost my height.
(A sheet slipped into the notebook:)
Russian science nearly suffered a tremendous loss.

CASE HISTORY ON PROFESSOR F.F. PREOBRAZHENSKY

At 1.13, Professor Preobrazhensky fell into a deep faint. Falling, he struck his head on a chair leg. Tincture of valerian.
In my presence and Zina's, the dog (if he can be called a dog, that is) rudely cursed Professor Preobrazhensky's mother.
(Break in notes.)
6 January (alternating pencil and violet ink).
Today, after his tail fell off, he said completely clearly "beer hall". Using the phonograph recorder. What the hell is this!!
I am at a loss!
No more office hours. Starting at 5 p.m. coming from the examining room, where this creature strolls about, clear vulgar cursing and the words "another pair".
7 January. He says many words: "coachman", "no room", "evening gazette", "the best present for children", and all the swear words that exist in the Russian lexicon.
He looks strange. Fur remains only on the head, chin and chest. The rest is bald with flabby skin. In the area of genitals, a man is forming. The skull has enlarged significantly, the forehead sloping and low.
I swear to God I will go mad.
Filipp Filippovich is still feeling poorly. I do most of the observations (phonograph, photographs).
Rumours are spreading throughout the city.
The consequences are incalculable. Today the whole street was full of wastrels and old women. The gawkers are still standing under our windows. The morning papers had an amazing report: "Rumours of a Martian in Obukhov Lane are baseless. They are being spread by merchants on Sukharevka and they will be severely punished." What Martian, damn it? It's a nightmare!!
It's even better in the *Evening Gazette*—they wrote that an infant was born that plays the violin. There's a drawing of the violin and my photograph and the caption: "Prof. Preobrazhensky, who performed the Caesarean on the mother." This is... indescribable... His new word: "policeman".
Turns out, Darya Petrovna was in love with me and stole my photo from F.F.'s album. After I chased out the reporters, one sneaked into the kitchen, and so on.
What goes on during office hours! There were 82 calls today. The telephone is unplugged. Childless ladies have gone mad and are coming...
The BuildCom headed by Shvonder. Why they came, they don't know themselves.

8 January. Late this evening, we came up with the diagnosis. F.F., like a true scientist, admitted his mistake—replacing the pituitary gland does not yield rejuvenation but complete humanization (*underlined three times*). This does not in any way lessen his astonishing, amazing discovery.

That one walked around the apartment today for the first time. He laughed in the corridor, looking at the electric light. Then, accompanied by Filipp Filippovich and myself, he continued into the study. He is steady on his hind (*crossed out*) legs and looks like a small and poorly built man.

He laughed in the study. His smile is unpleasant and somehow artificial. Then he scratched his head, looked around, and I took down a new, clearly enunciated world: "bourgeois". He swore. His swearing is methodical, ceaseless and, apparently, completely meaningless. It bears a rather phonographic character: as if this creature had heard swear words somewhere, automatically and unconsciously recorded them in his brain, and was now bringing them up in packets. But, of course, I'm not a psychiatrist, damn it!

The cursing has a surprisingly depressive effect on Filipp Filippovich. There are moments when he escapes his restrained and cold observation of new phenomena and seems to lose his patience. Thus, during the cursing, he suddenly shouted nervously: "Down!"

This had no effect.

After the walk in the study, with our joint efforts Sharik was forced back into the examining room.

After that Filipp Filippovich and I had a conference. This is the first time, I must admit, that I have seen this confident and astonishingly intelligent man at a loss. Humming as usual, he asked, "What will we do now?" And he replied himself, literally this way: "MoscTailor, yes... 'From Seville to Granada.' MoscTailor, dear doctor." I understood nothing. He explained, "I am asking you, Ivan Arnoldovich, to buy him linens, trousers and a jacket."

9 January. His vocabulary is enriched every five minutes (on average) by a new word and, since this morning, phrases. It seems that they were frozen in his consciousness and are thawing and coming out. The new words remain in use. Since yesterday, I have recorded on the phonograph: "don't push", "beat him", "scoundrel", "get off the step", "I'll show you", "American acclaim" and "primus".

10 January. The dressing took place. He permitted the undershirt readily, even laughing merrily. He refused the underpants, expressing his protest with hoarse cries: "Get in line, you sons of bitches, get in line!" He was dressed. The socks are too big.

(Schematic drawings in the notebooks, apparently depicting the transformation of a dog's leg into a human one.)

The back half of the foot skeleton (Tarsus) lengthens. The toes extend. Claws.

Repeated systematic training on visiting toilet.

The maid is completely depressed.

But the creature's comprehension must be noted. Things are moving in the right direction.

11 January. He's completely accepted trousers. Said a long, cheerful phrase, touching Filipp Filippovich's trousers: "Gimme a smoke, your pants are a joke."

The fur on his head is weak and silky. Easily confused with hair. But the spots remain on his temples. Today the last of the fuzz wore off his ears. Colossal appetite. Enjoyed the herring.

At five o'clock an event: for the first time, the words spoken by the creature were not at a remove from surrounding events but were a reaction to them. To wit, when the professor ordered, "Don't throw bones on the floor," he responded unexpectedly, "Shove off, pal!"

F.F. was astonished, then collected himself and said, "If you ever dare to swear at me or the doctor, you will be punished."

I photographed Sharik at that moment. I swear that he understood the professor's words. A sullen shadow fell over his face. He looked up in irritation from beneath his brows, but he quietened down.

Hurrah, he understands!

12 January. Putting hands in pockets. Training him not to curse.

He whistled 'Oh, Little Apple'. *

Holds up his end of a conversation.

I can't refrain from several hypotheses: the hell with rejuvenation for now! The other is immeasurably more important: Professor Preobrazhensky's amazing experiment has revealed one of the secrets of the human brain! Now the mysterious function of the pituitary gland—the brain's appendage—has been clarified! It determines the human image! Its hormones can be called the most important in the organism—the hormones of image! A new area in science is opened: without using Faust's retort a homunculus is created! The surgeon's scalpel brought a new human unit into life! Professor Preobrazhensky, you are a creator!!!

(Ink blot)

But, I digress... And so, he holds up his end of a conversation. As I see it, this is the situation: the transplanted pituitary gland opened the speech centre in the dog's brain, and the words gushed in torrents. I think that we are seeing a revived, developed brain and not a newly created brain. O, marvellous confirmation of the theory of evolution! O, the great chain from dog to Mendeleyev the chemist!*

Here is another of my hypotheses: Sharik's brain in the canine period of his life accumulated a ton of concepts. All the words that he used first were street words which he had heard and kept in his brain. Now, walking down the street, I look at dogs with hidden horror. God only knows what's in their brains!

Sharik can read. Read!!! (*Three exclamation marks.*) I was the one to guess it! From Glavryba! He read it backwards from the end! And I even know where the solution to this puzzle lies: in the decussation of the dog's optic nerves!

What's going on in Moscow is beyond human comprehension! Seven Sukharevsky merchants have been imprisoned for spreading rumours about the doomsday brought on by the Bolsheviks. Darya Petrovna said and even named the date: 28 November 1925, the day of St Stefan the Martyr, the Earth will hit the heavenly axis!! Some swindlers are already giving lectures. We've created such a hullabaloo with that pituitary that I just want to flee the apartment! I've moved into Preobrazhensky's at his request and I sleep in the reception room with Sharik. The examining room has been turned into the reception. Shvonder was right. The BuildCom is gloating. There are no panes left in any of the cupboards, because he was jumping. We barely taught him to stop.

Something terrible is happening to Filipp. When I told him about my hypotheses and my hope to develop Sharik into a psychologically elevated individual, he snorted and replied, "Really?" His tone was vicious. Could I be mistaken? The old man has come up with something. While I struggle with the case history, he pores over the case history of the man whose pituitary gland we removed.

(Inserted sheet in the notebook.)

Klim Grigoryevich Chugunkin, 25. Bachelor. No party membership, a sympathizer. Tried three times and acquitted: the first time because of lack of evidence; the second, his origins saved him; and the third, he got a suspended sentence of 15 years' hard labour. Theft. Profession: playing the balalaika in taverns. Short, poorly built. Swollen liver (alcohol). Cause of death—stabbed in the heart at the Stop Signal Bar near the Preobrazhenskaya Gate.

The old man sits with Klim's chart without cease. I don't understand the point. He muttered something about not having had the sense to examine Chugunkin's entire body at the morgue. I just don't understand! Does it matter whose pituitary gland it is?
17 January. I haven't made notes in several days: had influenza.
Over that time, the image has formed completely:

a) completely human in body;
b) weight around 100 lbs;
c) short stature;
d) small head;
e) has started smoking:
f) eats human food;
g) dresses independently;
h) converses fluently.
That's some pituitary! (*Blot.*)
Herewith I end the medical history. Before us is a new organism, and it must be observed from the beginning.
Attachments: transcripts of speech, phonograph recordings, photographic pictures.
Signed: assistant to Professor F.F. Preobrazhensky,

Doctor Bormental

Chapter 6

It was a winter evening. Late January. Before dinner, before office hours. A sheet of white paper hung on a hook by the door to the reception room, on which was written in Filipp Filippovich's hand:

I forbid eating sunflower seeds in the apartment.

F. Preobrazhensky

And in blue pencil with letters as large as pastries, in Bormental's hand:

Playing musical instruments between the hours of 5 p.m. and 7 a.m. is forbidden.

Then in Zina's hand:

When you get back, tell Filipp Filippovich: I don't know where he went. Fyodor said he was with Shvonder.

In Preobrazhensky's hand:

Will I have to wait a hundred years for the glazier?

In Darya Petrovna's hand (block letters):

ZINA WENT TO THE STORE, SHE SAID SHE WOULD BRING HIM.

The dining room felt completely like evening, thanks to the lamp with the silk shade. The light from the buffet sideboard fell broken in half—the mirrored panes were taped in an angled cross from one facet to the other. Filipp Filippovich, bent over the table, was immersed in the enormous sheet of the unfolded newspaper. Flashes of lightning distorted his face and fragmented, broken, grumbling words slipped through his teeth. He read the notice:

There is no doubt that he is his illegitimate (as they used to say in the rotten bourgeois society) son. That is how our pseudo-scientific bourgeoisie amuses itself! Each one knows how to occupy seven rooms until the gleaming sword of justice shines above him in a red beam.

Shv—r

A balalaika was playing very persistently and with a dashing agility two rooms away, and the sounds of a clever variation on 'The Moon Is Shining' mixed in Filipp Filippovich's head with the words from the newspaper into a hateful mush. When he finished reading, he spat dryly over his shoulder and unthinkingly sang through his teeth: "'The mooooon is shining... Shining... the moon is shining...' Pfui... it's stuck in my brain... damned tune!"

He rang. Zina's face showed between the drapes.

"Tell him it's five o'clock. Time to stop. And call him here, please."

Filipp Filippovich sat in an armchair by the table. A brown cigar stub stuck out from between the fingers of his left hand. By the drapes, leaning against the lintel, one leg behind the other, stood a short man with an unpleasant appearance. The hair on his head was bristly, like shrubs on a ploughed field, and there was unshaven fluff on his face. His brow was astonishingly low. The thick brush of hair began almost directly above the black tassels of his widespread eyebrows.

His jacket, torn under the left arm, was sprinkled with straw, the right knee of the striped trousers was ripped and the left smeared with purple paint. Around his neck, the little man wore a tie of a toxic sky colour with a fake ruby pin. The colour of that tie was so bright that from time to time, shutting his weary eyes, Filipp Filippovich could see in total darkness a blazing torch with a blue flame on the ceiling or the wall. Opening them, he was blinded anew by the sight of patent-leather lace-up shoes with white spats spraying fountains of light from the floor.

"Like galoshes," thought Filipp Filippovich with an unpleasant feeling, sighed, huffed, and began fussing with the cigar that had gone out. The man in the doorway regarded the professor with murky eyes and smoked a *papirosa*,* scattering ash on his shirt front.

The clock on the wall next to the wooden hazel grouse struck five. Something inside the clock was still groaning when Filipp Filippovich embarked on a conversation.

"I believe I've asked you twice now not to sleep on the plank bed by the stove in the kitchen, especially in the daytime?"

The man coughed hoarsely, as if choking on a bone, and replied, "The air is more pleasant in the kitchen."

His voice was unusual, soft yet resonant, as if in a small barrel.

Filipp Filippovich shook his head and asked, "Where did you get that vile thing? I'm speaking of the tie."

The man, following the pointing finger, squinted over his pouting lip and looked lovingly at the tie.

"Why 'vile'?" he said. "It's a fabulous tie. Darya Petrovna gave it to me."

"Darya Petrovna gave you a vile thing. Like those shoes. What is that glowing nonsense? From where? What did I request? Buy de-cent shoes! And what is this? Could Doctor Bormental have picked those out?"

"I told him to get patent leather. What, am I worse than other people? Go out on Kuznetsky, everyone's wearing patent leather."

Filipp Filippovich turned his head and spoke significantly: "Sleeping on the kitchen bed is ended. Understood? What obnoxiousness! You are in the way! There are women there."

The man's face darkened and his lips stuck out.

"Some women! Big deal! Fancy ladies! An ordinary servant and she acts like a commissar. It's that Zinka tattling."
Filipp Filippovich gave him a stern look. "Don't you dare call Zina 'Zinka'! Do you understand?"
Silence.
"Do you understand, I said?"
"I understand."
"Remove that thing from your neck. You... just take a look at yourself in the mirror—you're a sight! A circus act! No throwing butts on the floor, I'm telling you for the hundredth time. I don't want to hear another swear word in the apartment. No spitting. There's the spittoon. Be careful at the urinal. No talking to Zina at all! She complains that you lurk in the dark waiting for her. Watch it! Who told a patient 'The dog only knows'? Do you think you're in a tavern?"
"You're really putting the squeeze on me, Pops," the man said plaintively.
Filipp Filippovich reddened and his spectacles gleamed. "Who here is a 'pops' to you? What familiarity! I never want to hear that word again! Use my name and patronymic when you address me!"
A presumptuous expression flashed in the man. "You and your rules... don't spit, don't smoke... don't go there... What is all this? It's just like being on the tram. Why won't you let me live? And it won't work about the 'pops', you know! Did I ask to have the surgery?" the man barked in outrage. "Fine behaviour! Grabbed an animal, sliced up his head, and now you mock him. Maybe I didn't give my permission for the surgery. And maybe, neither did (the little man looked up at the ceiling, as if trying to recall a formulation), neither did my family. Maybe I have the right to sue."
Filipp Filippovich's eyes grew completely round and the cigar fell from his hands. "What a character!" flew through his mind.
"What," he asked, narrowing his eyes, "you dare to be displeased to have been turned into a human? Perhaps you would prefer to run around the rubbish dump again? Freeze in the alleys? Well, had I but known!"
"Why do you keep berating me with the dump? I was earning my crust! What if I had died under your knife? What do you have to express about that, Comrade?"
"'Filipp Filippovich!'" Filipp Filippovich exclaimed in irritation. "I'm no comrade of yours! This is monstrous!" He thought, "A nightmare, a nightmare!"

"Yes, of course, we understand," said the man ironically and victoriously set his foot back. "We understand! How could we be comrades! No way! We weren't educated in universities or brought up in fifteen-room apartments with bathrooms! But now it is time to drop all that. At the present time, everyone has the right—"

Filipp Filippovich turned pale as he listened to the man's ruminations. The latter interrupted his speech and demonstratively headed towards the ashtray carrying his chewed *papirosa*. He had a swaying gait. He crushed the butt in the tray for a long time, his expression clearly saying: "Take that! And that!" Having put out the *papirosa*, he suddenly clicked his teeth and stuck his nose under his arm.

"Catch fleas with your fingers! Your fingers!" shouted Filipp Filippovich furiously. "And I can't understand where you get them."

"What do you think, that I breed them or something?" The man was insulted. "Apparently, fleas like me," he said, feeling around in the lining under his sleeve and releasing a clump of reddish cotton batting into the air.

Filipp Filippovich turned his gaze to the garlands on the ceiling and drummed his fingers on the table. The man executed the flea and moved away to sit on a chair. He let his hands dangle from the wrists along the lapels of his jacket. His eyes squinted towards the squares of the parquet floor. He was admiring his shoes, which gave him great pleasure. Filipp Filippovich glanced down at the harsh glints of light on the squared toes, narrowed his eyes, and spoke. "What other matter did you want to report to me?"

"Some matter! It's a simple matter. I need a document, Filipp Filippovich."

A nerve twitched on Filipp Filippovich's face.

"Hm... Damn... A document! Really... Hm... Well, maybe it can be avoided somehow?" His voice was unconfident and bleak.

"Oh, please," the man replied confidently. "How can one be without a document? Well, excuse me. You know that a person is strictly forbidden to exist without a document. First of all, the BuildCom!"

"What does this BuildCom have to do with it?"

"What do you mean, what? They run into me, they ask, 'When are you going to register, esteemed one?'"

"Oh, my God," exclaimed Filipp Filippovich drearily. "'Run into you, they ask...' I can imagine what you tell them! Don't forget that I have forbidden you to skulk around the stairs!"

"What am I, a convict?" the man demanded, and the consciousness of his righteousness burned even in his ruby. "What do you mean 'skulk'? Your words are rather offensive! I walk like everyone else."

He slid his patent-leathered feet along the floor.

Filipp Filippovich grew silent and averted his eyes. "I really need to control myself," he thought. He went to the buffet and gulped down a glass of water.

"Fine," he said more calmly, "it's not about the words. So, what does this charming BuildCom of yours say?"

"What is there to say? And you needn't berate it as 'charming'. It defends interests."

"Whose interests, may I enquire?"

"You know whose. The labouring element."

Filipp Filippovich's eyes bulged. "How are you a labourer?"

"You know I'm not a NEPman."*

"Well, all right. Thus, what does it need to defend your revolutionary interests?"

"You know what: register me. They say it's impossible for a man to live in Moscow unregistered. That's one. But the most important thing is a registration card. I don't want to be a deserter. And then, the union, the exchange—"

"Would you please tell me where I'm supposed to register you? On this tablecloth? On my own passport? You have to consider the situation! Don't forget that you... er... hm... you are, so to speak, an unexpected creature, a laboratory..." Filipp Filippovich spoke with dwindling confidence.

The man maintained a victorious silence.

"Excellent. What then is needed, really, in order to register you and generally arrange things according to the plan of this BuildCom of yours? After all, you have no name or surname!"

"You're being unfair. I can select a name for myself quite easily. Just print it in the newspaper, and wham! Presto!"

"And what do you wish to be called?"

The man adjusted his tie and replied, "Polygraf Polygrafovich."

"Stop playing the fool," Filipp Filippovich responded sourly. "I'm being serious with you."

A sarcastic smirk twisted the man's little moustache.

"I seem to be missing something here," he said merrily and meaningfully. "I can't swear, I can't spit, and all I hear from you is 'fool' and 'fool'. Apparently, only professors are allowed to swear in the RSFSR."*

Blood rushed to Filipp Filippovich's head, and as he poured water into a glass, he broke it. Drinking from another, he thought, "A little more and he'll start lecturing me and he'll be absolutely right. I can't control myself anymore."

He bowed with exaggerated politeness and with iron firmness in his voice he said, "For-give me. My nerves are shot. Your name seemed strange to me. I wonder where you dug it up?"

"The BuildCom suggested it. They looked in the calendar,* which one do you want, and I picked it."

"There couldn't be anything of the sort in any calendar."

"That's rather surprising," the man chuckled, "since it's in your examining room."

Filipp Filippovich leant back without getting out of his chair to the button on the wallpaper, and Zina appeared in response to the ring.

"The calendar from the examining room."

A pause ensued. When Zina returned with the calendar, Filipp Filippovich asked, "Where?"

"He's celebrated on 4th March."

"Show me... Hm... damn... Into the stove with it, Zina, right now!"

Zina, eyes bulging in fear, left with the calendar, and the man shook his head reproachfully.

"May I know your surname?"

"I'm willing to take my hereditary surname."

"What? Hereditary? That is?"

"Sharikov."

Chairman of the BuildCom Shvonder, in a double-breasted leather jacket, stood in front of the desk in the study. Doctor Bormental sat in the armchair. The doctor's frost-reddened cheeks (he had just returned) bore the same bewildered expression as Filipp Filippovich.

"What should be written?" he asked impatiently.

"Why," Shvonder said, "it's not complicated. Write an affidavit, Citizen Professor. That, like, the holder of this is indeed Citizen Sharikov, Polygraf Polygrafovich, hm... conceived in your, like, apartment—"

Bormental, surprised, shifted in his chair. Filipp Filippovich's moustache twitched.

"Hm... what the hell... I can't imagine anything stupider than this. He wasn't conceived at all, but simply... well, basically—"

"That's your problem," Shvonder said with calm gloating, "whether he was conceived or not... The whole point is that you did the experiment, Professor! So you created citizen Sharikov."

"It's really simple," barked Sharikov from the bookcase. He was peering at his tie, reflected in the mirrored abyss.
"I would beg you," Filipp Filippovich snarled, "not to interfere in the conversation. You are wrong to say 'It's really simple'—it is really not simple."
"How can I not interfere?" Sharikov muttered in an injured tone, and Shvonder instantly supported him.
"Forgive me, Professor, Citizen Sharikov is completely correct. It is his right to participate in the discussion of his own fate, especially since the matter concerns documents. A document is the most important thing in the world."
At that moment, a deafening ring above his ear broke off the conversation. Filipp Filippovich said into the receiver, "Yes!" reddened and shouted, "I ask that you not distract me with trifles! What's it to you?" And he whipped the receiver into the cradle.
An idyllic joy spread over Shvonder's face.
Filipp Filippovich, turning crimson, shouted, "Let's finish this."
He tore a sheet out of a pad and scribbled a few words, which he read aloud in irritation.
"'I hereby attest'... damned if I know what this is... Hm... 'The bearer is a person, obtained by laboratory experiment via an operation on the brain, who needs documents'... Damn!... I am against you obtaining these idiotic documents!... 'Signed: Professor Preobrazhensky.'"
"It's rather strange, Professor," Shvonder said, taking umbrage, "how can you call documents idiotic? I cannot allow the habitation in our building of an undocumented resident, especially one who has not been put on the army draft list by the police. What if there is a war with imperialist predators?"
"I'm not going to any war," Sharikov barked grimly into the bookcase.
Shvonder was taken aback but quickly regained his position and noted obligingly to Sharikov, "You, Citizen Sharikov, are speaking unconsciously in the highest degree. You must be on the military list."
"I'll go on the list, but fight—you can go blow," Sharikov replied with hostility, adjusting the bow.
It was Shvonder's turn to be confused. Preobrazhensky looked over at Bormental both viciously and sadly, "Fine morals, eh?" Bormental nodded significantly.
"I was heavily wounded during the operation," Sharikov whined grimly. "See what they did to me?" He pointed to his head. A very fresh surgical scar stretched across his brow.

"Are you an anarchist individualist?" Shvonder asked, eyebrows rising high.
"I should have a medical exemption," Sharikov responded to that.
"Well, that's not important right now," replied the astounded Shvonder. "The fact is that we will send the professor's affidavit to the police and you will be given a document."
"Here's the thing, uh..." Filipp Filippovich interrupted, clearly tormented by some thought or other, "would you have a free room in the building? I'm willing to buy it."
Yellow sparks appeared in Shvonder's brown eyes. "No, Professor, to my great regret. No possibility of one."
Filipp Filippovich compressed his lips and said nothing. The phone rang like mad again. Filipp Filippovich, without answering it, silently threw the receiver from the cradle so hard that it spun a bit and then dangled on its light-blue cord. Everyone shuddered.
"The old man's nerves are shot," thought Bormental, while Shvonder, eyes gleaming, bowed and left.
Sharikov, the leather borders of his shoes creaking, followed him out.
The professor was left alone with Bormental. After a short time, Filipp Filippovich shook his head rapidly and began speaking. "It's a nightmare, upon my word. Do you see? I swear, dear Doctor, these last two weeks have been more exhausting than the last fourteen years! He's a character, I'll tell you—"
In the distance, glass smashed softly, then a stifled female scream flew up and immediately went out. An evil spirit raced across the wallpaper in the hallway, heading for the examining room, where something crashed, and instantly flew back again. Doors slammed and Darya Petrovna's low cry resounded in the kitchen. Then Sharikov howled.
"My God! What now!" shouted Filipp Filippovich, rushing to the door.
"A cat," surmised Bormental and rushed out behind him. They ran down the corridor to the entrance, burst in, from there turned down the corridor to the toilet and bathroom. Zina jumped out of the kitchen and bumped right into Filipp Filippovich.
"How many times have I given the orders, no cats!" Filipp Filippovich shouted furiously. "Where is he? Ivan Arnoldovich, calm down the patients in the reception, for God's sake!"
"In the bathroom, the damned devil is in the bathroom," Zina shrieked, panting.
Filipp Filippovich shoved against the bathroom door, but it did not yield.
"Open up this second!"

In response, something jumped around the locked bathroom walls, knocking over basins, and Sharikov's wild voice roared mutedly beyond the door: "I'll kill you on the spot!"
Water rushed through the pipes and poured out. Filipp Filippovich pushed harder on the door and began tugging at it. Overheated Darya Petrovna, her face contorted, appeared in the kitchen doorway. Then the high glass pane, leading from the bathroom to the kitchen at ceiling level, crashed with a vermiform crack and two shards fell from it, followed by a huge cat with tiger stripes and a pale-blue ribbon on his neck, looking like a policeman. It fell right on the table onto the long serving dish, which broke in half lengthwise, leapt from the dish to the floor, then turned on three legs, raising the right one as if dancing, and instantly squeezed through a narrow crevice onto the back stairs. The crevice expanded, and the cat was replaced by an old lady's phizog in a kerchief. The old woman's skirt, sprinkled with white polka dots, appeared in the kitchen. The old woman wiped her concave mouth with her index finger and thumb, cast her puffy and prickly eyes around the kitchen, and said with curiosity, "Oh, Lord Jesus!"
Pale Filipp Filippovich crossed the kitchen and asked the old woman sternly, "What do you want?"
"I'd like a look at the talking dog," the old woman replied beseechingly and crossed herself.
Filipp Filippovich grew even paler, came right up to the woman and whispered stiflingly, "Out of this kitchen this second."
The old woman backed towards the door and said in an injured voice, "You're awfully rude, Professor sir."
"Out, I say," repeated Filipp Filippovich, and his eyes grew as round as the owl's. He personally slammed the back door behind the old woman. "Darya Petrovna, haven't I asked you before?!"
"Filipp Filippovich," replied Darya Petrovna in despair, balling up her exposed hands into fists. "What can I do?... People keep trying to barge in all day, I'd have to drop everything else!"
The water in the bathroom roared dull and threatening, but no voices were heard. Doctor Bormental came in.
"Ivan Arnoldovich, I beg you... Hm... how many patients out there?"
"Eleven," Bormental replied.
"Let them all go, I won't see patients today!"
Filipp Filippovich rapped his knuckle on the door and shouted, "Come out this moment! Why have you locked yourself in?"
"Ooo-ooo!" Sharikov's voice was piteous and dull.

"What the hell!... I can't hear you! Turn off the water!"
"Woof... oooo!"
"Turn it off! What has he done? I don't understand!" shrieked Filipp Filippovich in a rage. Zina and Darya Petrovna, mouths agape, stared at the door in despair. A suspicious splashing joined the noise of the rushing water. Filipp Filippovich banged his fist on the door.
"There he is!" called Darya Petrovna from the kitchen.
Filipp Filippovich hurried there. In the broken window by the ceiling, Polygraf Polygrafovich's mug appeared and pushed through into the kitchen. It was contorted, the eyes weepy, and a scratch, flaming with fresh blood, extended along his nose.
"Have you lost your mind?" asked Filipp Filippovich. "Why aren't you coming out?"
Sharikov, also in despair and fear, looked around and replied, "I'm clicked in!"
"Open the lock! What, haven't you ever seen a lock?"
"It won't open, damn it," Polygraf replied fearfully.
"Lordy! He clicked the double lock!" cried Zina and clasped her hands.
"There's a little button," shouted Filipp Filippovich, trying to be heard over the water. "Push it down... Down! Push it down!"
Sharikov vanished and returned to the window in a minute.
"Too dark to see a dog in here," he barked in horror through the window.
"Turn on the light! He's gone mad!"
"Damned cat smashed the lamp," replied Sharikov, "so I started to grab the bastard by the legs, the tap got twisted off and now I can't find it."
All three clasped their hands before them and froze in that position.
About five minutes later, Bormental, Zina and Darya Petrovna were sitting next to each other on a wet rug rolled up at the bottom of the door, using their nether parts to press it against the crack under the door, while Fyodor the doorman, holding Darya Petrovna's wedding candle, climbed up the wooden ladder to the dormer window. His rear end in large grey checks flashed in the air and vanished into the opening.
"Wooof-oooo!" Sharikov shouted something through the roar of the water.
Under pressure, water sprayed a few times onto the kitchen ceiling and then grew still.
Fyodor's voice could be heard: "Filipp Filippovich, we have to open the door anyway, let it flow out, we'll pump it out of the kitchen!"
"Open!" cried Filipp Filippovich angrily.

The troika stood up from the rug, the bathroom door was opened and a wave poured into the hallway. There, it separated into three streams: straight into the toilet opposite, right to the kitchen and left to the entrance. Sloshing and hopping, Zina slammed the door to the entrance. Ankle-deep in water, Fyodor came out, smiling for some reason. He looked as if he had been wrapped in oilcloth—all wet.
"Barely shut it off, the pressure is strong," he explained.
"Where is he?" Filipp Filippovich asked and raised one foot with a curse.
"Afraid to come out," chuckling stupidly, Fyodor explained.
"Will you beat me, Pops?" came Sharikov's whiny voice from the bathroom.
"Idiot!" responded Filipp Filippovich succinctly.
Zina and Darya Petrovna, skirts tucked above the knee and bare-legged, and Sharikov and the doorman, barefoot with pants rolled up, swabbed the kitchen floor with wet rags, which they wrung out into dirty buckets and the sink.
The abandoned stove hummed. Water went out the door to the back stairs right through the staircase, falling into the cellar.
Bormental, standing on tiptoe in a deep puddle on the parquet floor of the entrance, negotiated through the door opened on the chain.
"No doctors' hours today, the professor is unwell. Please, move away from the door, we had a burst pipe."
"When will he receive?" a voice behind the door demanded. "I just need a minute."
"I can't," Bormental said, rocking back from his toes onto his heels. "The professor is lying down, and the pipe is burst. Please, come back tomorrow. Zina, dear! Wipe away from here, otherwise it will pour out onto the front stairs."
"The rags won't take it!"
"We'll bail it out with mugs!" called Fyodor. "Coming!"
The doorbell kept ringing, and now Bormental's whole foot was in the water.
"Then when will the surgery be?" importuned a voice trying to push through the crack.
"The pipe burst."
"I can come in my galoshes."
Bluish silhouettes appeared beyond the door.
"Sorry, come back tomorrow."
"But I have an appointment."
"Tomorrow. We've had a catastrophe with the plumbing."

Fyodor squirmed around at the doctor's feet in the lake, bailing with a mug, while scratched-up Sharikov came up with a new method. He rolled a huge rag into a tube, lay down with his stomach in the water and pushed it from the entrance back towards the bathroom.
"You loon, why are you pushing it all through the apartment?" grumbled Darya Petrovna. "Pour it into the sink!"
"Forget the sink!" Sharikov replied, trying to catch the murky water with his arms. "It will crawl out onto the front stairs."
With a creak, a bench rolled out of the corridor with Filipp Filippovich in blue striped socks stretched out on it, balancing himself.
"Ivan Arnoldovich, stop answering. Go to the bedroom, I'll give you slippers."
"It's all right, Filipp Filippovich, it's nothing!"
"Get galoshes then!"
"Really, it's all right. My feet are wet anyway."
"Oh, my God," said Filipp Filippovich bleakly.
"What a vicious animal," Sharikov grumbled suddenly and came out squatting with a soup bowl in his hand.
Bormental slammed the door and gave in to laughter. Filipp Filippovich's nostrils flared and his glasses glinted.
"You are speaking of whom?" he asked Sharikov from on high. "Permit me to know."
"I'm talking about the cat. What a bastard!" Sharikov replied, eyes wandering.
"You know, Sharikov," Filipp Filippovich responded, after a deep breath, "I have positively never seen a more brazen creature than you."
Bormental giggled.
"You," Filipp Filippovich continued, "are obnoxious! How dare you say that! You are the cause of all this and yet you dare... No! The Devil knows what this is!"
"Sharikov, tell me, please," Bormental asked, "how much longer are you going to chase cats? Shame on you, it's outrageous, you know!"
"Savage!"
"I'm no savage!" Sharikov responded grumpily. "No savage at all. It's impossible to allow him in the apartment. He just looks for something to swipe. He gobbled up Darya's ground meat. I wanted to teach him a lesson."
"You need to be taught a lesson!" replied Filipp Filippovich. "Just look at your mug in the mirror."

"Almost lost an eye," Sharikov responded firmly, touching his eye with a black, wet hand.
When the parquet floor, so soaked it was black, had dried a bit and all the mirrors bore a steam-bath sheen and the doorbell had stopped ringing, Filipp Filippovich stood in the entrance wearing red leather slippers.
"This is for you, Fyodor."
"I thank you humbly."
"Change your clothes immediately. But wait: have Darya Petrovna give you some vodka."
"I thank you humbly," Fyodor shuffled his feet and then said, "There's something else, Filipp Filippovich. I apologize, I feel guilty. But there's the glass in apartment seven... Citizen Sharikov threw rocks..."
"At a cat?" asked Filipp Filippovich, darkening like a cloud.
"As if—at the apartment owner. He's threatening to go to court."
"Damn!"
"Sharikov embraced their cook, and the master started to chase him out... Well, they got into it..."
"Please, always tell me about such things right away. How much do you need?"
"One and half."
Filipp Filippovich fished out three shiny fifty-copeck coins and handed them to Fyodor.
"Having to shell out that much on account of that bastard," came the low voice from the doorway. "It's all his—"
Filipp Filippovich turned, bit his lip, and silently pushed Sharikov into the reception room and locked him in. Sharikov instantly started banging his fists on the door.
"Don't you dare!" Filipp Filippovich cried in a sickly voice.
"Well, that's really something," Fyodor noted meaningfully. "I've never seen anyone so obnoxious in my life!"
Bormental appeared out of nowhere. "Filipp Filippovich, I beg you, stay calm!" The energetic Asclepius* unlocked the door to the reception room, and they could hear his voice coming from there. "What's the matter with you? Do you think you're in a tavern or something?"
"That's the way!" Fyodor added enthusiastically. "That's it! And box his ear too!"
"Now, now, Fyodor," Filipp Filippovich muttered sadly.
"Believe me, I feel sorry for you, Filipp Filippovich."

Chapter 7

"No, no, and no!" Bormental began insistently. "Please tuck it in!"
"Really, what, honest to God," grumbled Sharikov.
"Thank you, Doctor," Filipp Filippovich said gently, "I've got tired of correcting him."
"I won't let you eat until you tuck it in. Zina, receive the mayonnaise from Sharikov."
"What do you mean, 'receive'?" Sharikov was upset. "I'll tuck it in now."
With his left hand he blocked the dish from Zina and with his right he shoved a napkin inside his collar, coming to resemble someone at the barber's.
"Use the fork, please," Bormental added.
Sharikov gave a long sigh and started fishing for pieces of sturgeon in the thick sauce.
"A little more vodka?" he announced interrogatively.
"Haven't you had enough?" Bormental enquired. "You've been hitting the vodka too much lately."
"Do you begrudge it?" Sharikov enquired and looked up from beneath his brow.
"That's silly," Filipp Filippovich interjected severely, but Bormental interrupted him. "Don't worry, Filipp Filippovich, I'll handle it. You, Sharikov, speak nonsense and the most outlandish thing is that you say it with aplomb and confidence. Of course, I don't begrudge the vodka, especially since it's not even mine but Filipp Filippovich's. It's just that it's harmful. That's one, and two, you behave improperly as it is without it."
Bormental pointed to the taped-up buffet.
"Zina, dear, please give me some more fish."
Sharikov reached for the decanter in the meantime, and with a sidelong glance at Bormental, poured himself a shot.
"You must offer it to others," said Bormental, "and in this way: first to Filipp Filippovich, then to me, and finally for yourself."
A barely visible satirical smile touched Sharikov's lips, and he filled all the shot glasses.
"We have to do everything like on parade," he said. "Napkin here, tie there, and 'excuse me', and 'please', '*merci*', instead of doing it for real. We're tormenting ourselves the way they did under the tsarist regime."
"And what is 'for real', may I enquire?"

Sharikov did not respond to Filipp Filippovich, instead raising his glass and saying, "Here's wishing that everything—"
"And the same to you," Bormental replied with some irony.
Sharikov sloshed the vodka down his throat, frowned, brought a piece of bread to his nose, sniffed it and then swallowed it, his eyes brimming with tears.
"A stage," Filipp Filippovich suddenly said curtly and as if in a trance.
Bormental glanced at him in amazement. "Sorry?"
"A stage!" repeated Filipp Filippovich and shook his head bitterly. "There's nothing to be done about it! Klim!"
Bormental peered with extreme interest into Filipp Filippovich's eyes. "Do you suppose so, Filipp Filippovich?"
"No supposing about it. I'm certain."
"Could it..." began Bormental and stopped, glancing over at Sharikov.
The latter frowned suspiciously.
"*Später*,"* said Filipp Filippovich softly.
"*Gut*," replied his assistant.
Zina brought in the turkey. Bormental poured some red wine for Filipp Filippovich and offered it to Sharikov.
"I don't want any. I'd rather have some vodka." His face looked greasy, sweat beaded his brow, and he was cheerful. Filipp Filippovich also grew kinder after his wine. His eyes were clearer and he regarded Sharikov, whose black head sat in the napkin like a fly in sour cream, with greater condescension.
Bormental, feeling stronger, revealed a tendency towards action. "Well, and what shall we undertake this evening?" he enquired of Sharikov.
He blinked and replied, "We'll go to the circus, that's the best."
"The circus every day?" Filipp Filippovich remarked rather genially. "That's rather boring, it seems to me. If I were you I'd go to the theatre at least once."
"I won't go to the theatre," Sharikov said with hostility and made the sign of the cross over his mouth.*
"Hiccuping at the table spoils the appetite of others," Bormental informed him automatically. "Please forgive me... Why, actually, don't you like the theatre?"
Sharikov looked into his empty shot glass as if it were binoculars, thought, and pouted. "It's tomfoolery... Talk and talk... Nothing but counter-revolution!"

Filipp Filippovich threw himself against the Gothic chair back and laughed so hard that gold palings sparkled in his mouth. Bormental merely shook his head.

"You should read something," he proposed, "otherwise, you know—"

"I'm reading and reading as it is," Sharikov replied and suddenly poured himself half a glass of vodka swiftly, like a predator.

"Zina!" Filipp Filippovich called anxiously. "Take the vodka away, child, we don't need any more! What are you reading?" He had a sudden picture flash through his mind: an uninhabited island, a palm tree, and a man in an animal skin and hat. "You should read Robinson—"

"That... whatchacallit... correspondence between Engels and that... what's his name, damn it... and Kautsky."*

Bormental's fork with a piece of white meat stopped halfway, and Filipp Filippovich spilt his wine. Sharikov managed to down his vodka in the meantime.

Filipp Filippovich rested his elbows on the table, looked at Sharikov and asked, "Permit me to enquire what you can say in connection with your reading."

Sharikov shrugged.

"I don't agree."

"With whom? Engels or Kautsky?"

"Both of them," Sharikov replied.

"Marvellous, I swear to God! 'All who say another!...'* And what would you propose instead?"

"What's there to propose?... They keep writing and writing... Congress, some Germans... makes my head ache! Just take everything and divide it up."

"Just as I thought!" exclaimed Filipp Filippovich, smacking the tablecloth with his hand, "That's just what I thought!"

"Do you know the method as well?" Bormental asked, intrigued.

"What method?" Sharikov had become more talkative under the influence of the vodka. "It's no secret. Look now: one is spread out over seven rooms, with forty pairs of pants, while another forages, looking for food in rubbish bins."

"The seven rooms is a dig at me, I take it?" Filipp Filippovich asked, narrowing his eyes haughtily. Sharikov huddled into himself and said nothing.

"Well, all right, I'm not against sharing. Doctor, how many patients did you turn away yesterday?"

"Thirty-nine people,' Bormental replied instantly.

"Hm... Three hundred and ninety roubles. Well, let the men bear the damage. We won't count the ladies—Zina and Darya Petrovna. Your share, Sharikov, is one hundred and thirty roubles. Please hand it over."

"A fine thing," replied Sharikov in a fright, "what's all this?"

"For the tap and the cat!" barked Filipp Filippovich, losing his state of ironic calm.

"Filipp Filippovich!" Bormental exclaimed anxiously.

"Wait! For the outrage you created, which made us cancel office hours! It is unacceptable! A man leaping around the apartment, like a savage, tearing off taps!... Who killed Madam Polasukher's cat? Who—"

"You, Sharikov, the other day you bit a lady on the stairs!" attacked Bormental.

"You stand—" growled Filipp Filippovich.

"She smacked me on the face!" screeched Sharikov. "My mug isn't public property!"

"Because you pinched her breast," shouted Bormental, knocking over his wine glass. "You stand—"

"You stand on the lowest step of development!" Filipp Filippovich out-shouted him. "You are a creature still in formation, weak mentally, all your actions are purely animal, and you, in the presence of two people with a university education, permit yourself with totally unbearable aplomb to offer advice of cosmic scale and equally cosmic stupidity on dividing everything up, and at the same time you gobbled up the tooth powder!"

"The other day," Bormental confirmed.

"So now," thundered Filipp Filippovich, "I will rub your nose in this... by the way, why did you wipe off the zinc oxide from it?... You will be silent and listen to what you are told! Learn and try to become at least a minimally acceptable member of society. By the way, what scoundrel outfitted you with that book?"

"You think everyone's a scoundrel," Sharikov replied fearfully, overwhelmed by the two-sided attack.

"I can guess!" exclaimed Filipp Filippovich, wrathfully turning red.

"Well, all right, then... Well, it was Shvonder. He's not a scoundrel. For my development—"

"I can see how you're developing after Kautsky," Filipp Filippovich shrieked, turning yellow. He furiously pushed the button on the wall. "Today's incident shows that better than anything! Zina!"

"Zina!" yelled Bormental.

"Zina!" screamed frightened Sharikov.

Zina ran in, pale.
"Zina, in the reception room... Is it in the reception room?"
"In the reception," Sharikov replied docilely. "Green, like vitriol."
"A green book—"
"He's going to fire off now!" Sharikov exclaimed in despair. "It's not mine, it's from the library!!"
"The correspondence is called... what's his name?... Engels with that devil... Into the stove with it!"
Zina turned and flew out.
"I would hang that Shvonder from the nearest tree, upon my word," Filipp Filippovich exclaimed, furiously clamping his teeth into a turkey wing, "this incomparable rotten creature exists in the building like a boil. It's not enough that he writes libellous nonsense in the papers..."
Sharikov squinted angrily and ironically at the professor. Filipp Filippovich in turn glared narrowly at him and stopped talking.
"Oh, nothing good will come of us here in the apartment," Bormental suddenly thought prophetically.
Zina brought in a round tray holding a baba, reddish on the right side and rosy on the left, and the coffee pot.
"I won't eat that," Sharikov announced in a threatening and hostile way.
"No one's asking you to. Behave yourself. Doctor, please."
The dinner ended in silence.
Sharikov pulled a crumpled *papirosa* from his pocket and lit up. Finishing his coffee, Filipp Filippovich looked at his watch, pressed the chimes, and they tenderly played quarter-past eight. Filipp Filippovich leant back on the Gothic chair as was his habit and reached for the newspaper on the side table.
"Doctor, please, take him to the circus. But, for God's sake, check the programme—are there any cats?"
"How can they let that kind of riff-raff into the circus," Sharikov noted grimly, shaking his head.
"They let all sorts in," Filipp Filippovich replied ambiguously. "What are they playing?"
"At Solomonovsky's," Bormental started reading, "there are four of these... Yussems and some kind of spinning man."
"What are Yussems?" Filipp Filippovich enquired suspiciously.
"God knows, I've never seen the word before."
"Well, then, you'd better see what Nikitin has. Everything must be clear."
"Nikitin... Nikitin... hm... Elephants and the extreme of human agility."

"Sooooo. What do you have to say regarding elephants, dear Sharikov?" Filipp Filippovich asked Sharikov doubtfully.
He was offended. "What, you think I don't understand, is that it? Cats are different, but elephants are useful animals," Sharikov replied.
"Fine then. If they're useful, then go and see them. You must obey Ivan Arnoldovich. And do not get into any conversations at the buffet. Ivan Arnoldovich, I humbly entreat you not to offer beer to Sharikov."
Ten minutes later, Ivan Arnoldovich and Sharikov, dressed in a duckbill cap and thick woollen overcoat with the collar turned up, left for the circus. It grew quiet in the apartment. Filipp Filippovich appeared in his study. He lit the lamp under the heavy green hood, which made the enormous study very peaceful, and started pacing the room.
The cigar tip burned long and hot with a pale-green fire. The professor tucked his hands into his trouser pockets and a heavy thought tormented his learned brow with its widow's peak. He smacked his lips, hummed, "To the sacred banks of the Nile," and muttered something.
At last, he set the cigar in the ashtray, went over to the cupboard that was completely made of glass, and illuminated the entire study with three powerful lights from the ceiling. From the third glass shelf in the cupboard, Filipp Filippovich removed a narrow jar and examined it, frowning, holding it up to the light. In the transparent and viscous liquid there floated, without sinking to the bottom, a small white lump, excised from the depths of Sharikov's brain. Shrugging, twisting his lips and hemming, Filipp Filippovich devoured it with his eyes, as if trying to find in the white, unsinkable lump the cause of the astonishing events that had turned life upside down in the apartment on Prechistenka.
It is quite possible that the scholarly man did find it. At least, having regarded to his content the appendage of the brain, he put away the jar, locked the cupboard, placed the key in his vest pocket and collapsed, tucking his head into his shoulders and sticking his hands deep into his jacket pocket, onto the leather of the couch. He burned a second cigar for a long time, chewing up its tip, and finally, in total solitude, coloured green like a grey-haired Faust, he exclaimed: "I swear to God, I think I'll do it!"
No one responded. All sounds had ceased in the apartment. Traffic stops in Obukhov Lane at eleven, as you know. Once in a great while the distant footsteps of a late pedestrian could be heard, thumping somewhere beyond the drapes, and then dying away. The pocket-

watch chimes rang gently beneath Filipp Filippovich's fingers in his pocket. The professor waited impatiently for Doctor Bormental and Sharikov to return from the circus.

Chapter 8

It's not known what Filipp Filippovich had decided to do. He did not undertake anything special in the course of the week and perhaps, in consequence of his inaction, everyday life in the apartment was overwhelmingly eventful.

About six days after the business with the water and the cat, the young man who turned out to be a woman from the BuildCom came to Sharikov and handed him documents, which Sharikov immediately placed in his jacket pocket and just as immediately afterwards called Doctor Bormental.

"Bormental!"

"Oh, no, you use my name and patronymic with me, please!" replied Bormental, face contorted.

It should be noted that in those six days the surgeon managed to argue some eight times with his charge, and the atmosphere was sticky in the rooms on Obukhov Lane.

"Then you use my name and patronymic," Sharikov replied quite reasonably.

"No!" thundered Filipp Filippovich in the doorway. "I will not permit you to be called by that name and patronymic. If you prefer not to be called familiarly as 'Sharikov', then Doctor Bormental and I will call you 'Mr Sharikov'."

"I'm not a mister, the misters are all in Paris," barked Sharikov.

"Shvonder's work!" shouted Filipp Filippovich. "Well, fine then, I'll deal with that scoundrel. There will be nothing but misters in my apartment as long as I live here! Otherwise, either you or I will leave here, and most likely that will be you! Today I will place an advertisement in the papers, and believe me, I'll find you a room!"

"Right, like I'm stupid enough to move from here," Sharikov replied very clearly.

"What?" demanded Filipp Filippovich and his face changed so much that Bormental rushed over and tenderly and anxiously took him by the sleeve.

"Don't you take liberties, Monsieur Sharikov." Bormental's voice was raised very high. Sharikov stepped back, pulled three papers from his pocket—green, yellow and white—and jabbing his fingers at them, said, "There. I'm a member of the residence association, and I'm assigned thirty-five square feet of space in apartment number five of the responsible renter Preobrazhensky." Sharikov thought and added

an expression that Bormental mechanically noted as new: "Be so kind."
Filipp Filippovich bit his lip and carelessly muttered through it, "I swear that I will end up shooting that Shvonder."
Sharikov took those words extremely attentively and acutely, as was apparent from his eyes.
"Filipp Filippovich, *vorsichtig*,"* Bormental began to caution him.
"Really, that's too... To stoop so low!" exclaimed Filipp Filippovich in Russian. "Bear in mind, Sharikov... Mr... that if you permit yourself one more obnoxious statement, I will deprive you of dinner and any board at all in my house. Thirty-five feet is delightful, but those froggish papers don't oblige me to feed you, do they?"
Sharikov was frightened and opened his mouth. "I can't stay without board," he muttered. "Where will I get grub?"
"Then behave yourself decently," both Asclepiuses howled as one.
Sharikov was significantly subdued and that day caused no harm to anyone except himself: using Bormental's brief absence, he appropriated his razor and ripped open his cheekbone so that Filipp Filippovich and Doctor Bormental had to give him stitches, which made Sharikov howl for a long time, weeping copiously.
The next night, two men sat in the professor's study in the dim green light—Filipp Filippovich and his loyal and devoted Bormental. Everyone else was asleep. Filipp Filippovich wore his azure robe and red slippers and Bormental was in shirtsleeves with blue suspenders. Between the doctors, the round table held a thick album, a bottle of brandy, a plate of lemon slices* and a cigar box. The scientists, having filled the room with smoke, were heatedly discussing the latest events: that evening Sharikov had stolen two ten-rouble notes lying under a paperweight from Filipp Filippovich's study, vanished from the apartment, returned late and completely drunk. More than that, he came back with two unknown characters who made noise on the front stairs and expressed their desire to spend the night as Sharikov's guests. The signified characters left only when Fyodor, who was present at this scene in his autumn coat thrown over his underwear, called the forty-fifth police station. The characters left the moment Fyodor hung up. With their departure, the malachite ashtray from the mirror shelf in the entrance, Filipp Filippovich's beaver hat and his walking stick, inscribed in gold with: "To dear and esteemed Filipp Filippovich from his grateful orderlies on the day..." followed by the Roman numeral XXV, went missing somewhere.
"Who are they?" Filipp Filippovich threatened Sharikov, making fists.

Swaying and sticking to the fur coats, he muttered that he did not know those characters and that they weren't some sons of bitches but good fellows.

"The most amazing part is that they were both drunk, how did they manage?" wondered Filipp Filippovich, regarding the spot on the stand where once stood the memorial of his anniversary.

"Specialists," explained Fyodor, heading back to bed with a rouble in his pocket.

Sharikov categorically and stubbornly denied the two ten-rouble notes and said something unclear about the fact that, like, he's not the only one in the apartment.

"Aha, perhaps it was Doctor Bormental who swiped the money?" enquired Filipp Filippovich in a voice quiet yet terrible in its tone.

Sharikov reeled, opened his completely owlish eyes and offered a suggestion: "Maybe Zinka took it."

"What!" screamed Zina, appearing in the doorway like a ghost, covering the unbuttoned blouse on her chest with her palms. "How dare he—"

Filipp Filippovich's neck turned red. "Easy, Zinusha," he said, extending a hand towards her. "Don't worry, we will take care of all this."

Zina immediately started wailing, blubbering, and her hand jumped up and down on her collarbone.

"Zina! Shame on you! Who could possibly think that? Pfui, how vile," Bormental said in confusion.

"Really, Zina, you're stupid, God forgive me," Filipp Filippovich began.

But Zina's weeping stopped of its own accord and everyone stopped talking. Sharikov was feeling sick. Hitting his head on the wall, he emitted a sound—not quite "ee" and not quite "eh"—like "eee-eh"! His face paled and his jaw worked convulsively.

"The bucket from the examining room for the scoundrel!"

Everyone ran around, taking care of the sick Sharikov. When they took him to bed, he stumbled in Bormental's arms and cursed very delicately and melodically with swear words, pronouncing them with difficulty.

This whole business had occurred around one o'clock, and now it was around three, but the two men in the study were wide awake, agitated by the brandy. They had smoked so much that the smoke moved in thick, slow layers without any swaying.

Doctor Bormental, pale, with a very determined gaze, raised a glass with a wasp waist. "Filipp Filippovich!" he exclaimed emotionally, "I'll never forget how I came to you, a half-starved student, and you sheltered me in the faculty. Believe me, Filipp Filippovich, you are much more to me than my teacher, my professor... My unlimited respect for you... Permit me to kiss you, dear Filipp Filippovich."

"Yes, my dear fellow, my..." Filipp Filippovich muttered in bewilderment and rose to meet him. Bormental embraced him and kissed him in his fluffy, heavily smoky moustache.

"I swear to God, Filipp Fili—"

"I'm so touched, so touched... thank you," Filipp Filippovich said. "My dear fellow, I sometimes shout at you during surgery. Do forgive an old man's irritability. Essentially, I am so alone... 'From Seville to Granada...'"

"Filipp Filippovich, you should be ashamed!" exclaimed fiery Bormental sincerely. "If you do not wish to offend me, do not speak to me in that manner."

"Well, thank you... 'To the sacred banks of the Nile!'... Thank you. And I've come to love you as a talented physician."

"Filipp Filippovich, I'm telling you," Bormental cried passionately, leapt from his chair, shut the door leading to the corridor more tightly, and continued in a whisper when he returned, "it's the only way. I don't dare give you advice, of course, but Filipp Filippovich, look at yourself, you're completely exhausted, you can't work any more!"

"Absolutely impossible!" Filipp Filippovich confirmed with a sigh.

"There, it's just unthinkable," whispered Bormental. "The last time you said that you were worried for me, and if you only knew how much that touched me, dear Professor. But I'm not a boy and I understand myself how terribly it might turn out. But, I profoundly believe that there is no other way."

Filipp Filippovich rose, waved his arms at him and exclaimed, "Don't tempt me, don't even say it." The professor paced the room, setting off smoky waves. "I won't even listen. You realize what will happen if we're discovered. We won't get off because 'class origins are taken into account', despite a previous conviction. We don't have the right origins, do we, dear boy?"

"Not in the least! My father was a judicial investigator in Vilno," Bormental replied bitterly, finishing his cognac.

"There, that won't do. It's a bad heredity. Can't even think of anything more disgusting. Actually, my mistake, mine's even worse. My father was an archpriest in a cathedral. *Merci*... 'From Seville to Granada in the quiet twilight...' Damn it all!"

"Filipp Filippovich, you are a luminary of world significance, and over some son of a bitch, pardon the expression... They wouldn't dare touch you, believe me!"
"All the more reason why I won't do it," Filipp Filippovich responded thoughtfully, stopping and looking at the glass cupboard.
"Why not?"
"Because you aren't a luminary of world significance."
"Far from it..."
"Exactly. But abandoning a colleague in case of catastrophe while getting out of it myself using my world significance, sorry... I am a Moscow student, not a Sharikov." Filipp Filippovich proudly straightened his shoulders and looked like an ancient French king.
"Filipp Filippovich, ah!" Bormental exclaimed bitterly. "Then what now? Put up with it? You're going to wait until we manage to turn that hooligan into a man?"
"Ivan Arnoldovich, in your opinion, do I understand a little in the anatomy and physiology of, say, the apparatus of the human brain? What do you think?"
"Filipp Filippovich, how can you ask!" Bormental replied with great feeling and opened his arms.
"Fine, then. Without false modesty. I also think that I'm not the last person in that area in Moscow."
"I think that you are the first, and not only in Moscow, but in London and Oxford too!" Bormental interrupted fiercely.
"Fine, so be it. But then listen, future Professor Bormental: No one can do it. No need to ask. Just use me as a reference. Tell them, Preobrazhensky said so. *Finita*! Klim!" Filipp Filippovich suddenly exclaimed triumphantly, and the cupboard responded with ringing panes. "Klim!" he repeated. "Here's the thing, Bormental, you're the best student in my school and besides that my friend, as I have become convinced today. So I am telling you a secret as a friend—of course I know that you will not shame me, how the old ass Preobrazhensky screwed up this operation like a third-year student. Of course, there was the discovery, you know that for yourself"—and here Filipp Filippovich pointed bitterly with both hands at the window shade, apparently indicating Moscow—"but just bear in mind, Ivan Arnoldovich, that the only result of this discovery will be that now we all will have that Sharikov up to here." Preobrazhensky patted himself on his bent neck, which had a tendency towards paralysis. "Don't worry! If someone," Filipp Filippovich continued voluptuously, "were to lay me down and give me a whipping, I swear I would pay him fifty

roubles! 'From Seville to Granada...' Damn me... I spent five years digging out appendages from brains... Do you know what kind of work I did, it's mind-boggling. And now I ask, for what? So that one fine day I could turn a sweet dog into scum that makes your hair stand on end!"
"Something exceptional."
"I don't agree at all. This is what happens, Doctor, when a researcher doesn't feel his way in parallel with nature but forces the issue and raises the curtain! Here, have your Sharikov and eat him with buckwheat!"
"Filipp Filippovich, what if it had been Spinoza's brain?"*
"Yes!" barked Filipp Filippovich. "Yes! If only the miserable dog doesn't die under the knife, and you've seen what sort of operation it is. In other words, I, Filipp Preobrazhensky, have never done anything harder in my life. One can transplant Spinoza's pituitary or that of some other supernatural creature and create from a dog something extremely high on the scale, but what the devil for, I ask? Explain to me, please, why we need to artificially fabricate Spinozas, when any peasant woman can give birth to one whenever!... After all, Mrs Lomonosov gave birth to her famous son in Kholmogory.* Doctor, humanity takes care of this itself, and in the evolutionary process, stubbornly separating out from the mass of all kinds of scum, it creates dozens of outstanding geniuses who ornament the globe. Now you see, Doctor, why I denigrated your conclusion in Sharikov's case history. My discovery, may the devils take it, which you think is so wonderful, isn't worth a plugged copeck... Don't argue, Ivan Arnoldovich, I've figured it out. I never waste my breath, you know that perfectly well. Theoretically, it is interesting, yes. Physiologists will be delighted... Moscow is in an uproar... But, practically, what do we have? Whom do you see before you?" Preobrazhensky pointed in the direction of the examining room, where Sharikov slept.
"An exceptional rascal."
"But who is he? Klim, Klim," shouted the professor, "Klim Chugunkin!" (Bormental's mouth fell open.) "Here is what that is: two convictions, alcoholism, 'divide up everything', my hat and twenty roubles missing (here Filipp Filippovich recalled his anniversary walking stick and turned red)—a lout and a pig... Well, I'll find that stick. In other words, the pituitary gland is a closed chamber that determines a person's given character. Given! 'From Seville to Granada...'" Filipp Filippovich shouted, eyes rolling furiously, "And not generally human! It is the brain itself in miniature! I don't need it at all, the hell with it! I was concerned with something completely different: eugenics, improving

the human race. And I came across rejuvenation! Do you really think that I regenerate them for the money? I am a scientist, after all—"

"You are a great scientist, so there," said Bormental, gulping brandy. His eyes were bloodshot.

"I wanted to do a small experiment after I first extracted sex hormone from the pituitary two years ago. And instead of that, what has happened, oh my God! All those hormones in the pituitary, oh Lord... Doctor, I am facing a dead end of hopelessness, I swear I am lost."

Bormental suddenly rolled up his sleeves and said, squinting at his nose, "Then here's the thing, dear teacher, if you do not wish to do it, I will feed him arsenic at my own risk. The hell with the fact that my father was a judicial investigator. After all, it's your own experimental creature."

Filipp Filippovich calmed down, weakened, collapsed into his chair and said, "No, I will not permit it, dear boy. I am sixty years old, I can give you advice. Never commit a crime, no matter against whom. Live to an old age with clean hands."

"But my goodness, Filipp Filippovich, if that Shvonder works on him some more, think what he'll turn into? God, I'm only beginning to realize what that Sharikov could become!"

"Aha! Now you understand? I realized it ten days after the operation. But see here, Shvonder is the greatest fool of all. He doesn't realize that Sharikov is a much graver threat to him than to me. Right now, he's trying everything to pit him against me, without realizing that if someone decides to pit Sharikov against Shvonder, there will be nothing left of him but his horns and hooves."

"Just think of the cats! A man with The Heart Of A Dog!"

"Oh, no, no," Filipp Filippovich drew out his words. "You are making an enormous mistake, Doctor—for God's sake, don't calumny the dog. The cats are just temporary... It's a question of discipline and two or three more weeks. I assure you. In a month or so he'll stop attacking them."

"But why not now?"

"Ivan Arnoldovich, it's elementary, are you really asking? The pituitary isn't going to just hang in the air. It's grafted onto a dog's brain, after all; give it time to take. Sharikov is now manifesting only the remnants of the canine, and don't forget that the cats are the best of what he's been doing. You must realize that the true horror is that he no longer has The Heart Of A Dog but a human one. The worst of all of those that exist in nature."

Agitated to the extreme, Bormental tightened his strong, thin hands into fists, straightened his shoulders, and stated firmly, "It's over. I'll kill him!"

"I forbid it!" Filipp Filippovich was categorical.

"Please—"

Filipp Filippovich looked up warily, raising his finger. "Wait... I heard footsteps."

They both listened, but it was quiet in the corridor.

"I imagined it," said Filipp Filippovich and spoke heatedly in German. The Russian word "criminality" sounded several times in his speech.

"Just a minute," Bormental suddenly said and stepped towards the door. Steps could be heard clearly, moving toward the study. In addition, a voice mumbled. Bormental flung open the doors and jumped back in astonishment. Completely stunned, Filipp Filippovich froze in his chair.

In the illuminated rectangle of the hallway, Darya Petrovna in just her nightgown stood with a militant and blazing face. The doctor and the professor were blinded by the abundance of the powerful and, as it seemed to the startled men, completely naked body. With her mighty arms, Darya Petrovna was dragging something, and that something resisted, sitting on its rear, and its small legs, covered with black fluff, struggled on the floor. The something was of course Sharikov, completely lost, still tipsy, dishevelled and in his night shirt.

Darya Petrovna, magnificent and naked, shook Sharikov like a sack of potatoes and said these words: "Take a look, Professor sir, at our visitor Telegraf Telegrafovich. I've been married, but Zina is an innocent girl. It's a good thing that I woke up."

Finishing this speech, Darya Petrovna fell into a state of shame, cried out, covered her bosom with her hands and rushed away.

"Darya Petrovna, forgive me, for Heaven's sake!" red-faced Filipp Filippovich, rousing himself, called after her.

Bormental rolled his shirtsleeves higher and moved on Sharikov.

Filipp Filippovich, seeing his eyes, was horrified. "Doctor! I forbid it."

Bormental grabbed Sharikov by the back of his shirt with his right hand and shook him so hard that the fabric on the back cracked and a button from the neck in front broke off.

Filipp Filippovich tried to head him off and began pulling scrawny Sharikov out of the tenacious surgical hands.

"You don't have the right to fight," half-stifled Sharikov shouted, sitting down on the floor and sobering up.

"Doctor!" screamed Filipp Filippovich.

Bormental came to his senses a bit and released Sharikov, who immediately started sobbing.
"Fine, then," hissed Bormental. "We'll wait until morning. I'll throw him a special benefit performance when he sobers up."
Then he grabbed Sharikov under his arms and dragged him to the reception room to sleep. Sharikov made an attempt to kick him away, but his legs would not obey.
Filipp Filippovich spread his feet, thus separating the azure skirts of his robe, raised his arms and eyes to the ceiling lamp in the corridor and said, "Well-well-well."

Chapter 9

The special performance for Sharikov promised by Doctor Bormental did not take place, however, the next morning because Polygraf Polygrafovich had vanished from the house. Bormental was infuriated and despairing, called himself an ass for not hiding the key to the front door, shouted that this was unforgivable, and ended with the hope that Sharikov would be hit by a bus. Filipp Filippovich sat in his study, hands in his hair, saying, "I can just imagine what will happen on the street... I can ima-a-gine. 'From Seville to Granada', oh, my God."

"He might still be in the BuildCom office," Bormental raged and ran off somewhere.

At the office he got into such an argument with chairman Shvonder that the latter sat down to write a complaint to the People's Court of Khamovnichesky District, shouting that he was not the keeper of Professor Preobrazhensky's ward, especially since that ward Polygraf no later than last night proved to be a fraud who took seven roubles from the committee allegedly to buy textbooks at the co-op store.

Fyodor, who had made three roubles on this incident, searched the house from top to bottom. There was no trace of Sharikov.

The only thing they learnt was that Polygraf had left at dawn wearing cap, scarf and coat, taking a bottle of ashberry vodka from the buffet, Doctor Bormental's gloves and all his documents. Darya Petrovna and Zina did not conceal their turbulent joy and hope that Sharikov would never return. Sharikov had borrowed three roubles and fifty copecks from Darya Petrovna the day before.

"Serves you right!" roared Filipp Filippovich, brandishing his fists.

The telephone rang all day, and the telephone rang the next day. The doctors saw an unusual number of patients, and on the third day the question arose firmly in the study about informing the police, who would have to find Sharikov in the whirlpool that was Moscow.

No sooner was the word "police" pronounced than the reverential quiet of Obukhov Alley was sundered by the barking of a truck, and the windows of the house shook. Then came a confident peal of the bell, and Polygraf Polygrafovich appeared in the entrance. Both the professor and the doctor came out to meet him.

Polygraf entered with extraordinary dignity, removed his cap in total silence, hung his coat on the coat rack and stood before them in a new guise. He wore a second-hand leather jacket, worn leather pants and tall English boots that laced to the knee. Preobrazhensky and Bormental, as if given a command, crossed their arms on their chests

and stood in the doorway, awaiting the first announcement from Polygraf Polygrafovich.
He smoothed his bristly hair, coughed and looked around, showing that Polygraf wanted to hide his embarrassment by overfamiliarity.
"I, Filipp Filippovich," he began at last, "have taken a position."
Both doctors made a vague dry sound in the throat and stirred.
Preobrazhensky was first to rouse himself and he reached out and said, "Give me the paper."
It read: "The bearer Comrade Polygraf Polygrafovich Sharikov is indeed head of the Subdepartment for Control of Moscow's Stray Animals (cats and so on) in the Department of Moscow Communal Administration."
"So," said Filipp Filippovich heavily, "who found you the job? Ah, actually, I can guess..."
"Well, Shvonder," replied Sharikov.
"Permit me to enquire why you give off that disgusting reek?"
Sharikov worriedly sniffed his jacket.
"Well, what can I do, it smells... obviously. From my speciality. Yesterday we killed and killed cats."
Filipp Filippovich shuddered and looked at Bormental. His eyes were like two black pistol barrels pointed directly at Sharikov. Without any preamble, he moved towards Sharikov and easily and confidently took him by the throat.
"Help!" Sharikov squeaked, turning pale.
"Doctor!"
"I won't do anything bad, Filipp Filippovich, don't worry," Bormental replied in a steely voice and then shouted, "Zina and Darya Petrovna!"
They appeared in the entrance.
"Repeat after me," said Bormental and pushed Sharikov's throat slightly towards the fur coat. "Forgive me..."
"All right, I'm repeating," Sharikov, completely vanquished, replied in a hoarse voice, and then suddenly took a deep breath, jerked away and tried to shout, "Help!" but the shout did not come out and his head was completely engulfed by the coat.
"Doctor, I beg you!"
Sharikov nodded to show that he was submitting and would repeat.
"...Forgive me, esteemed Darya Petrovna and Zinaida—"
"Prokofyevna," Zina whispered in fright.
"Prokofyevna," Sharikov said hoarsely, gasping for air.
"...that I permitted myself..."
"...permitted..."

"...vile behaviour at night in a state of intoxication..."
"...intoxication..."
"I will never do it again..."
"...will ne—"
"Let him go, let him go, Ivan Arnoldovich," both women entreated simultaneously. "You'll choke him!"
Bormental released Sharikov and said, "Is the truck waiting for you?"
"No," Polygraf replied respectfully. "It just brought me here."
"Zina, tell the car to leave. Now bear this in mind: you have returned to Filipp Filippovich's apartment?"
"Where else could I go?" Sharikov replied meekly, eyes darting.
"Fine. Keep quiet, lie low. Otherwise, you will have me to deal with for every outrageous act. Understood?"
"Understood," Sharikov replied.
Filipp Filippovich had said nothing during the violence on Sharikov. He had huddled pathetically near the door lintel and chewed on his nail, gaze directed at the floor. Then he looked up at Sharikov and asked, softly and mechanically, "What do you do with those... killed cats?"
"They'll go to make coats," Sharikov said. "They'll turn into 'squirrel' for worker credit."
Thereupon, silence descended upon the apartment and continued for two days. Polygraf Polygrafovich left in the morning by truck, returned in the evening, dined quietly in the company of Filipp Filippovich and Bormental. Despite the fact that Bormental and Sharikov slept in the same room, the reception, they did not speak to each other, and Bormental was first to tire of it.
About two days later, a thin young lady wearing eyeliner and cream stockings appeared in the apartment and was truly overwhelmed by its opulence. In her shabby coat she followed Sharikov and bumped into the professor in the entrance.
He stopped, stunned, squinted and asked, "May I be informed?"
"I'm registering marriage with her; she's our typist, she'll live with me. Bormental will have to move out of the reception room, he has his own apartment," Sharikov explained with extreme hostility and grumpiness.
Filipp Filippovich blinked, thought as he regarded the red-faced young lady, and spoke to her very courteously, "I'll ask you to come into my study for a minute."
"I'll go with her," Sharikov said quickly and suspiciously.

The decisive Bormental popped up instantly, as if from under the floor.
"Excuse me," he said. "The professor will chat with the lady, and you and I will wait here."
"I don't want to," Sharikov replied angrily, trying to follow the young lady, burning with shame, and Filipp Filippovich.
"No, sorry." Bormental took Sharikov by the arm and they went to the examining room.
For about five minutes, no sounds were heard from the study and then suddenly came the muffled sound of the young lady's weeping.
Filipp Filippovich stood by his desk, and the young lady cried into a dirty lace hankie.
"He said, the louse, that he was wounded in combat," the young lady sobbed.
"He's lying," Filipp Filippovich replied intransigently. He shook his head and continued, "I feel sincere sympathy for you, but really you can't just go off with the first person you meet, just for the sake of your job... Child, it's outrageous... Now here."
He opened a desk drawer and took out three thirty-rouble notes.
"I'll get food poisoning," the young lady wept. "The canteen serves salt beef every day... He threatened me, says he's a red commander... with me, he says, you'll live in a luxurious apartment... pineapple every day... my psyche is kind, he says, it's only cats I hate... he took my ring for a keepsake."
"Well, well, well, a kind psyche... 'From Seville to Granada'," muttered Filipp Filippovich. "You'll get over this, you're so young."
"Was it really in this very alley?"
"Come on, take money when it's offered, a loan," snapped Filipp Filippovich.
Then the doors were opened ceremoniously, and Bormental, at Filipp Filippovich's signal, brought in Sharikov. His eyes darted around, and the pelt on his head bristled like a brush.
"Scoundrel," said the young lady, flashing her puffy, smeared eyes and stripy powdered nose.
"Do explain to this lady why you have a scar on your forehead," Filipp Filippovich asked ingratiatingly.
Sharikov bet the house. "I was wounded at the front fighting Kolchak,"* he barked.
The young lady stood and left with a loud cry.
"Stop!" Filipp Filippovich called after her. "Wait! The ring," he said to Sharikov.

He obediently removed the hollow ring with an emerald.
"All right now," he said angrily to her, "you're in for it now. Tomorrow I'll arrange to have you fired!"
"Don't be afraid of him!" Bormental shouted after her. "I won't let him do anything." He turned and gave Sharikov a look that made him back away and bang his head on the cupboard.
"What's her surname?" Bormental asked him. "Her name!!!" he screamed, suddenly looking savage and terrifying.
"Vasnetsova," replied Sharikov, looking around for an escape route.
"Every day," Bormental said, holding the lapel of Sharikov's jacket, "I will personally enquire about staff reductions, whether Citizen Vasnetsova has been fired. And if you... if I find out that she's been fired, I will shoot you with my own hands that very moment! Watch it, Sharikov, I'm speaking to you in plain Russian!"
Sharikov stared at Bormental's nose.
"We'll find our own revolvers," Polygraf muttered, but very weakly, and then suddenly twisted away and shot out the door.
"Watch it!" Bormental's cry caught up with him.
That night and half the next day, silence hung in the air like a cloud before a storm. But everyone was silent. But the next day, when Polygraf Polygrafovich, who had felt a bad premonition that morning, left gloomily for work in the truck, Professor Preobrazhensky, at a totally unofficial time, saw one of his previous patients, a fat and tall man in military uniform. He had insisted on an appointment and got it. Entering the study, he clicked his heels politely.
"Have your pains returned, dear fellow?" asked the haggard Filipp Filippovich. "Sit down please."
"*Merci*. No, Professor," his visitor replied, placing his helmet at the corner of the desk, "I'm very grateful to you. Um... I'm here for something else, Filipp Filippovich... With my great respect... hm... To warn you. It's blatant nonsense. He's just a scoundrel."
The patient dug into his briefcase and took out a piece of paper. "It's a good thing they reported it to me directly."
Filipp Filippovich saddled his nose with pince-nez over his glasses and started reading. He muttered to himself for a long time, his face changing expression every second.
"...and also threatened to kill Chairman of the BuildCom Comrade Shvonder, which shows that he has firearms. And he makes counter-revolutionary speeches and even ordered his social servant Zinaida Prokofyevna Bunina to burn Engels in the stove, as a blatant Menshevik with his assistant Ivan Arnoldovich Bormental, who

without being registered lives secretly in his apartment. I certify the signature of Head of the Animal Control Subdepartment P.P. Sharikov. Chairman of BuildCom Shvonder, Secretary Pestrukhin."

"May I keep this?" asked Filipp Filippovich, all blotchy, "or, forgive me, perhaps you need this to set legal machinery in action?"

"Excuse me, Professor," said the patient in great offence, nostrils flaring, "you really do have a very scornful view of us. I—" and here he started puffing up like a turkey cock.

"Forgive me, forgive me, dear fellow," muttered Filipp Filippovich, "forgive me, truly I did not wish to insult you."

"We know how to read papers, Filipp Filippovich!"

"Dear fellow, don't be angry, he's driven me to distraction."

"I can imagine," the patient said, completely calm again. "But what scum he is! I'd be curious to see him. There are all sorts of legends going around Moscow about you."

Filipp Filippovich merely waved off the suggestion in despair. And here the patient saw that the professor had grown stooped and even seemed to have turned grey over recent months.

The crime ripened and fell like a stone, as it usually happens. With a festering feeling in his heart, Polygraf Polygrafovich returned in the truck. Filipp Filippovich's voice called him into the examining room. Surprised, Sharikov entered and with a vague fear looked at the gun barrels on Bormental's face and then at Filipp Filippovich. A dark cloud circled the assistant and his left hand, holding a cigarette, trembled on the shiny arm of the obstetric chair.

Filipp Filippovich said with very nasty calm, "Gather up your things now: trousers, coat, everything you need, and get out of the apartment."

"What do you mean?" Sharikov was truly surprised.

"Get out today," Filipp Filippovich repeated in a monotone, squinting at his fingernails.

Some evil spirit had entered Polygraf Polygrafovich; apparently disaster was waiting for him and fate was behind his back. He threw himself into the embrace of the inevitable and barked angrily and curtly, "What is this, really! Do you think I won't find a way to deal with you? I'm sitting on thirty-five feet here and I'm staying."

"Get out of the apartment," Filipp Filippovich whispered with feeling.

Sharikov invited his death. He raised his left hand and made a rude gesture with his bitten and cat-stinking finger at Filipp Filippovich. And then with his right hand, addressed to the dangerous Bormental, he took a revolver from his pocket. Bormental's *papirosa* dropped like a falling star and a few seconds later, Filipp Filippovich, horrified and jumping over broken glass, was rushing between the cupboard and the couch. There, prostrate and gasping, lay the head of the Animal Control Subdepartment, and on his chest was the surgeon Bormental, smothering him with a small white pillow.

A few minutes later, Doctor Bormental, his face unrecognizable, went to the front door and put up a sign next to the bell: "No patients today because the professor is ill. Please do not disturb by ringing the bell."

He used his shiny penknife to cut through the bell's wires, and then he examined his scratched, bloody face and his torn hands, jittering with a rapid tremor, in the mirror. Then he appeared in the kitchen doorway and in a cautious voice said to Zina and Darya Petrovna, "The professor asks that you do not leave the apartment."

"All right," replied Zina and Darya Petrovna meekly.

"Allow me to lock the back door and take the key," said Bormental, hiding in the shadows behind the door and covering his face with his hand. "It's temporary, and not out of lack of trust in you. But if someone comes, you won't be able to resist and you'll open up, and we can't be disturbed. We're busy."

"All right," the women replied and immediately turned pale.

Bormental locked the back door, locked the front door, locked the door from the corridor to the entrance, and then his steps vanished near the examining room.

Silence covered the apartment, crept into all the corners. Twilight crawled in, nasty, wary; in a word, gloom.

Of course, later the neighbours across the courtyard maintained that allegedly all the lights were on in Preobrazhensky's examining-room windows, which open on the yard, and that they even saw the professor's white cap...

Checking this is difficult. Of course, even Zina, when it was all over, gabbed that in the study, by the fireplace, after Bormental and the professor left the examining room, Ivan Arnoldovich had scared her to death. Allegedly he was crouched in the study by the fire burning his own notebook with the blue cover out of the pile in which he kept the case histories of the professor's patients. The doctor's face was allegedly completely green and completely, really completely scratched to bits. And Filipp Filippovich that night was not himself. And also... However, it's also possible that the naive girl from the apartment on Prechistenka is lying...

But one thing is definitely true. That night the apartment was filled with total and terrible quiet.

Printed in Great Britain
by Amazon

62532960R00050